GO GAMING!

THE ULTIMATE GUIDE TO THE WORLD'S GREATEST MOBILE GAMES

EDITOR IN CHIEF
Jon White

EDITOR
Stephen Ashby

WRITERS
Luke Albigés, Wesley Copeland, Jonathan Gordon,
Ross Hamilton, Oliver Hill, Ryan King, Simon Miller, Dominic Peppiatt,
Dominic Reseigh-Lincoln, Edward Smith, Paul Walker-Emig, Josh West

LEAD DESIGNER
Adam Markiewicz

DESIGNERS
Andy Downes, Andy Salter, Liam Warr, Jonathan Wells

PRODUCTION
Sarah Bankes, Sanne de Boer, Steve Holmes, Fiona Hudson, Jen Neal

ISBN 978-1-338-11811-7
10 9 8 7 6 5 4 3 2 1   17 18 19 20 21
Printed in the U.S.A.   40
First printing, January 2017

Scholastic is constantly working to lessen the environmental impact of our
manufacturing processes. To view our industry-leading paper procurement
policy, visit www.scholastic.com/paperpolicy.

STAYING SAFE AND HAVING FUN

If you're gaming on the go, the most important thing is to pay attention to your surroundings—always look where you're going. As with any gaming, check out a game's rating before you play it and if you're playing online with others, remember that they're not real-life friends. Here are some top tips:

1 Talk to your parents about what the rules are in your family, such as how long you can play games for, or what websites you can visit.

2 Don't download or install games or apps to any device, or fill out any forms on the Internet, without first checking with the person that the device belongs to.

3 Take regular breaks—putting your mobile device down every now and then is not only good for your eyes, it will also allow you to refresh and improve your play.

4 If you're playing games when you're on the move, be mindful of other people, and look where you're going.

5 Don't forget—games are meant to be fun! If things aren't going well in the game, just take a time out and come back to it later.

6 Don't respond to any online conversations that are mean or make you feel bad. Let your parents know right away.

7 Never agree to meet someone you met online in person, and never send photographs of yourself.

8 Don't feel pressured to spend money on games or apps. If a game tells you to spend money, speak to your parents.

9 When you're online, be nice to other people. Don't say or do anything that could hurt someone else's feelings or make them feel unhappy.

10 Never give out personal information such as your real name, phone number, password, or anything about your parents.

SKYLANDERS SUPERCHARGERS

You may have played it on Xbox One, PS4, or Wii U, but now *Skylanders* is also on tablet! And you can transport all your favorite Skylanders into the game, just like the console versions.

CONTENTS

FEATURES

8-17	**THE BEST MOBILE GAMES EVER**
18-21	BEST MOBILE-GAMING ACCESSORIES
24-25	**BEST PUZZLE GAMES**
28-29	SHOWCASE: LUMINO CITY
34-39	**BEST UNIQUE GAMES**
44-51	THE BEST FREE GAMES
56-59	**BEST SELF-IMPROVEMENT GAMES**
62-67	BIG GAMES ON THE SMALL SCREEN
68-69	**BEST LOCAL MULTIPLAYER GAMES**
70-71	BEST RHYTHM GAMES
74-75	**BEST ZOMBIE GAMES**
80-83	COOLEST CONTROL SYSTEMS
84-85	**SHOWCASE: MONUMENT VALLEY**
88-89	BEST RACING GAMES
90-91	**BEST JAPANESE GAMES**
98-101	RETRO GAMES REVISITED
104-105	**BEST VIRTUAL PET GAMES**
110-113	BIZARRE SPORTS GAMES
114-115	**SHOWCASE: RAYMAN ADVENTURES**
118-119	BEST VR GAMES
120-121	**TOP 8 AUGMENTED REALITY GAMES**
126-127	GLOSSARY

78

73

43

GAMES

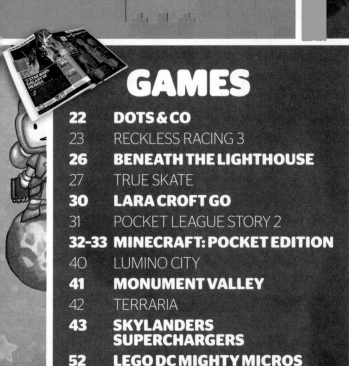

22	**DOTS & CO**
23	RECKLESS RACING 3
26	**BENEATH THE LIGHTHOUSE**
27	TRUE SKATE
30	**LARA CROFT GO**
31	POCKET LEAGUE STORY 2
32-33	**MINECRAFT: POCKET EDITION**
40	LUMINO CITY
41	**MONUMENT VALLEY**
42	TERRARIA
43	**SKYLANDERS SUPERCHARGERS**
52	**LEGO DC MIGHTY MICROS**
53	SONIC DASH 2: SONIC BOOM

54	**HEARTHSTONE: HEROES OF WARCRAFT**
55	STACK
60-61	**SLITHER.IO**
72	CANDY CRUSH SAGA
73	**RAYMAN ADVENTURES**
76	DROPSY
77	**FIELDRUNNERS 2**
78	SCRIBBLENAUTS REMIX
79	**MOMOKA: AN INTERPLANETARY ADVENTURE**
86	DISNEY CROSSY ROAD
87	**FTL: FASTER THAN LIGHT**
92-93	STAR WARS: GALAXY OF HEROES
94	**DON'T STARVE: POCKET EDITION**
95	JETPACK JOYRIDE
96	**BADLAND 2**
97	GEOMETRY WARS 3: DIMENSIONS
102	**PRUNE**
103	OCTODAD: DADLIEST CATCH
106	**RIPTIDE GP2**
107	ASPHALT 8: AIRBORNE
108	**TRIPLE TOWN**
109	THE SIMPSONS: TAPPED OUT
116	**CRASHLANDS**
117	MARVEL FUTURE FIGHT
122	**ANGRY BIRDS ACTION!**
123	THREES!
124	**TEMPLE RUN 2**
125	DESPICABLE ME: MINION RUSH

53

74

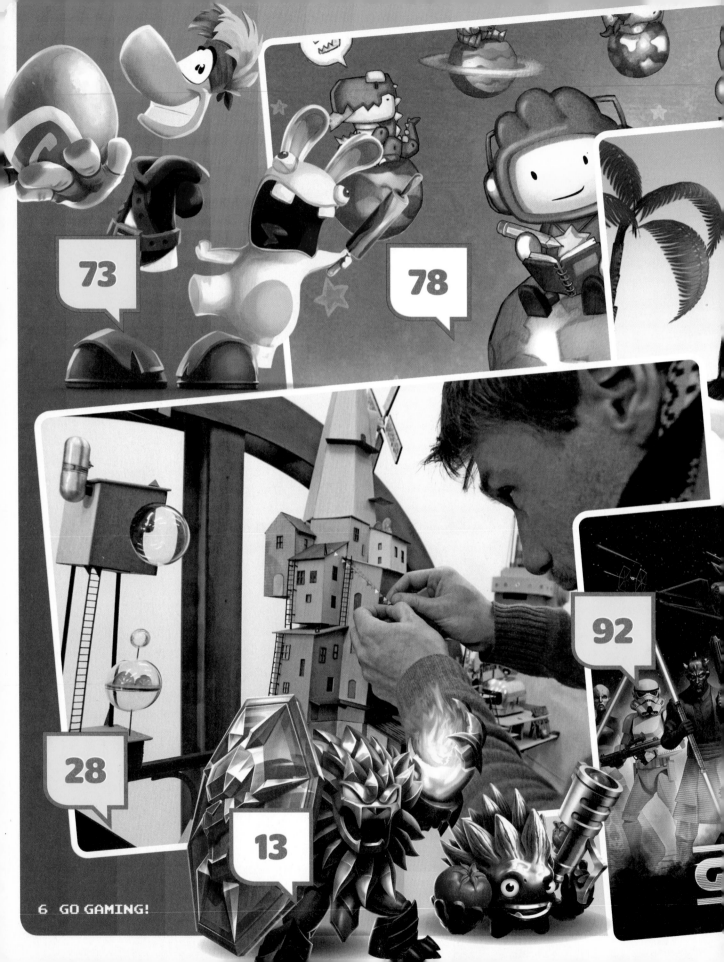

73

78

28

92

13

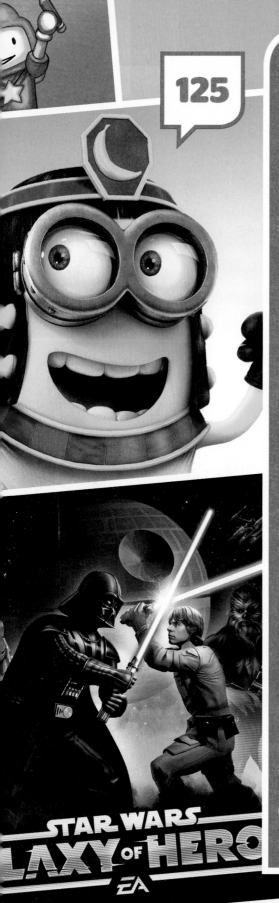

WELCOME TO

GO GAMING!

INCREDIBLE GAMING ON THE MOVE!

Even people who have never held a game controller in their lives have probably played some kind of mobile game. From *Crossy Road* and *Pokémon GO* to *Hearthstone* and *Candy Crush*, mobile gaming offers unique experiences that you just can't get anywhere else. Some are great for keeping busy for a few minutes on the bus, while others offer huge depth, massive worlds, and sprawling story lines that will draw you in for hours.

What's really awesome about mobile games is the sheer variety. Cool control methods let you tip and tilt your device to steer, tap the screen to attack, or even swing or shake your phone to jump around on screen. There are beautifully animated games like *Lumino City*, amazing puzzle games like *Monument Valley*, tough brainteasers like *Lara Croft GO,* and some of the weirdest games that you've ever played—we're looking at you, *Goat Simulator.* And that's why we love them so much. No matter what kind of game you're looking for, you're bound to find something you love that you can play on your smartphone or tablet. We've put together a collection of some of the very best games ever made for mobile devices, with hints, tips, tricks, and much more. You'll find a wealth of new titles to download and enjoy, but you might also find out more about games you already love.

THE BEST MOBILE GAMES EVER

39

BROKEN AGE

Featuring an all-star cast of voice actors, including Elijah Wood and Jack Black, *Broken Age* is a puzzle-packed point-and-click style adventure in which players can switch between two different characters to experience similar situations in different worlds. It's engrossing and very enjoyable.

MINECRAFT: STORY MODE

37

This hilarious adventure sees Jesse, a newbie Minecraft player, working with his friends to save the Minecraft world. You must tap on on-screen objects to explore familiar places like the Overworld and the Nether, choose what to say to the people you meet, and craft the tools you need to beat the evil Wither Storm.

38

FRUIT NINJA

It might be mindless, but *Fruit Ninja* is awesome fun. You just have to swipe your finger across the screen to carve up fruit that's being flung at you, as if you're wielding a ninja sword. You get bonus points for combos, and there are certain items, like bombs, that you have to avoid at all costs.

36

CARD WARS— ADVENTURE TIME CARD GAME

Inspired by the "Card Wars" episode of the *Adventure Time* TV show, this app has you drawing cards to command your own army of troops and destroy your opponent's forces. By using the right cards you can summon creatures and cast spells as you battle your way to glory. Featuring characters and the oddball humor from the TV show, this is a surprisingly engaging and exciting game to play with others.

34

WILLIAM

Perfect match!
You got
277
for a score of
10 points

CONTINUE

75 6 10 3 5 4

75 x 4 = 300
6 x 5 = 30
300 - 30 = 270
10 - 3 = 7
270 + 7 = 277

COUNTDOWN—THE OFFICIAL TV SHOW APP

Whether you watch and enjoy the UK TV show, or you just like forming words out of a random stream of letters, you will find this app good fun. It also features a math round to test your mental arithmetic, as well as the "Countdown Conundrum." It's a good way to wake up your brain and giving it a thorough workout.

35

CASTLE OF ILLUSION STARRING MICKEY MOUSE

Fondly remembered as a 90s console classic, *Castle of Illusion* has been tweaked and enhanced for its mobile release, and it looks incredible. Mickey has to run and jump through a variety of side-scrolling and 3-D levels, collecting treasure in a bid to save Minnie from the clutches of a vile witch.

33

TOUCHGRIND SKATE 2

If you find fingerboarding too tricky, then this is definitely the next best thing. You control the on-screen deck using your fingers, exactly as you would a fingerboard, and can pull off amazing tricks without sending a little plastic deck flying in random directions. There is much here to master and marvel at as you attempt to tame the terrain across a range of awesome skate parks.

FALLOUT SHELTER

A neat spin-off from the post-apocalyptic console adventures, *Fallout Shelter* has you building your dream bunker for your fallout survivors. You can search the wasteland for construction materials, radio out to attract new survivors, add a wide range of rooms, and assign jobs to keep everyone happy. It's kind of like a radioactive version of the *Sims* games!

32

TAMAGOTCHI CLASSIC

If you enjoy rearing and caring for virtual pets, this app version of the once-very-popular keychain toy contains all the elements you could possibly desire. Feed your pet, flush away its poop, and play a series of games to keep it happy and in prime health.

31

WARHAMMER QUEST

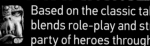

Based on the classic tabletop game, this app blends role-play and strategy. You lead your party of heroes through enemy-filled dungeons in search of treasure to plunder. The top-down view works perfectly, as all manner of unsavory creatures jump out from the darkness.

30

MACHINARIUM

Whoever thought that robots could love? This epic steampunk adventure follows Josef the robot as he attempts to rescue his kidnapped girlfriend from the clutches of the Black Cap Brotherhood gang. Along the way he has to interact with an oddball cast of characters, solve puzzles, and explore the slightly grimy surroundings. With plenty to see and do, *Machinarium* is a lot of fun to play, although it is lacking any sort of replay value.

29

28

TICKET TO RIDE

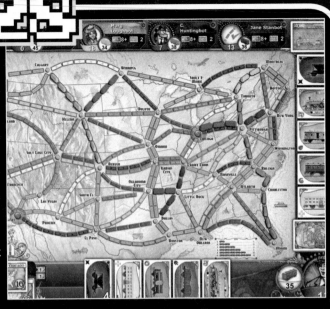

An app version of a classic strategy board game, the aim of *Ticket to Ride* is to connect railway routes between two locations that are kept secret from the other players. Featuring the same artwork and maps from the board game, it is great fun for kids, as well as for adult players who will fondly remember playing the original game.

FLICK GOLF!

One of the best mobile golf games around, *Flick Golf!* allows you to flick your balls towards the green, applying all kinds of curve and spin to get great results. Like the other "flick" games on the market, it is easy to master and very hard to put down.

27

Budget: 7100/17000

BRIDGE CONSTRUCTOR

If you like to think of yourself as an budding engineer, put your skills to the test in this bridge-building game. Here you have to choose the best materials to bridge gaps on the island of Camatuga, ensuring that they are capable of handling the daily flow of traffic. Let your imagination run wild as you design epic constructions, but whatever you do, don't go over budget.

26

REAL BOXING

Train hard and get on the road to glory by working your way up from obscurity to the big time. This easy-to-play boxing simulator lets you slug your opponents down to the mat with an array of dazzling moves, without breaking a sweat.

25

CANABALT

If you're in the mood for some intense platform action, *Canabalt* truly delivers. You are constantly confronted with challenging terrain, meaning you need to react quickly to deal with it—or die in the process. The awesome pick-up-and-play gameplay means this is one mobile game you are sure to keep returning to again and again.

24

REAL RACING 2

 Real Racing 2 proves that a thrilling driving game can work well on a touchscreen interface. You can work your way up from a rookie to a pro in "Career Mode," handle 30 officially licensed cars over 15 challenging tracks, and compete against 15 other cars as you jostle for the checkered flag.

23

PUNCH QUEST

An enjoyable, arcade-style scrolling beat-'em-up with a simple control method, *Punch Quest* has you punching your way through dungeons packed with monsters. In your quest you get to ride laser-shooting dinosaurs, turn into magical gnomes, and fully customize your character. What's not to like?

22

OSMOS

In this ultra chilled-out game you play a ball of light that has to grow and expand by absorbing other balls of light. It sounds relatively straightforward, right? Wrong, because before too long the levels get incredibly complicated as the other balls of light start to behave in new and different ways.

21

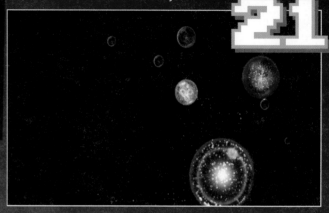

POKÉMON GO

This game sends users out into the real world to hunt down critters. Using your device's location data, this hugely popular game combines geocaching with classic Pokémon gameplay as you capture creatures and train them for combat. It's a great way of getting some exercise—and enjoying it!

19

SKYLANDERS TRAP TEAM

20

This was the first *Skylanders* game available to mobile gamers. You connect a specially adapted "Portal of Power" to your device and use your favorite Skylanders figures in-app as you battle through a variety of levels that feature platform and shooting action. You can use the same Skylanders with later games, too.

18

THOMAS WAS ALONE

As you might have guessed, this isn't your usual platforming game—in *Thomas Was Alone* you are a rectangle. You play through 100 levels of action to unravel the mysteries of your existence. The story is a lot more emotional and engaging than a tale about simple shapes has any right to be!

ANGRY BIRDS RIO

17

Released to coincide with the animated movie *Rio* in 2011, this game nicely evolves the *Angry Birds* series. It features cool new levels based on locations from the film and new birds who bring new abilities to the party. New levels are regularly added to the game, even several years after its release.

THE KING OF FIGHTERS-A 2012

16

With 34 different characters to master, each with their own unique array of screen-shattering special moves, this is an awesome fighting game with a simple control system. Within a few minutes of play you'll be stringing combo moves together like a seasoned pro. The only thing missing is online multiplayer.

WORLD OF GOO

Winner of numerous mobile gaming awards, *World of Goo* is a gloriously gloopy game in which you have to create structures, bridges, and objects out of goo balls to progress through the levels. Each level presents a new challenge, and new species of goo balls are introduced as you go to keep you enthralled.

14

FLIGHT CONTROL

Air traffic control isn't easy. All those planes requesting permission to land, running low on fuel, and needing guidance to land safely. This stressful job is conveyed excellently in *Flight Control*. Utilize great multitasking skills to land as many aircraft as possible, from passenger planes and private jets to helicopters.

15

80 DAYS **13**

Part story, part interactive adventure, you take on the role of Phileas Fogg's personal assistant as he embarks on an epic journey to travel around the world in 80 days. Manage your resources, plan routes, and organize transportation, ensuring that Fogg reaches home in time to win a bet, just like in Jules Verne's original novel.

LIFELINE: **12** WHITEOUT

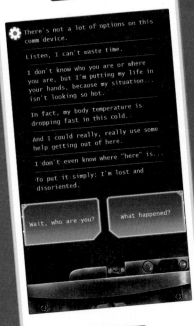

A gripping and enthralling text-based adventure, you are the last hope for this lost adventurer, who you must guide back to safety. What's amazing is that the game uses your phone's built-in services to provide real-time notifications as if what you are playing is happening in real life. If you want to try something a bit different, this is it!

FLICK KICK FOOTBALL

Experience the sensation of curling a free kick into the top corner of the net, just like Ronaldo and Beckham, with this insanely addictive finger soccer game. Apply the power and curve by flicking your finger across the ball. Aim to beat the goalkeeper—not to mention an assortment of statuesque defenders.

11

ANGRY BIRDS STAR WARS **10**

If you ever thought you'd get sick of *Angry Birds* games, this app will show you how wrong you are. Injecting fresh humor and the familiarity of the *Star Wars* films, this game brings a star destroyer-full of new levels, as well as hilarious bird-based variants of the characters we know and love.

9

THE ROOM THREE

All *The Room* games are worth checking out, but this is the most recent. It follows the theme of a mystery that needs solving by cracking complex puzzles, searching for clues, and fully exploring your surroundings. Atmospheric and engrossing, once you get caught up in the intrigue it is very hard to put down.

PAC-MAN

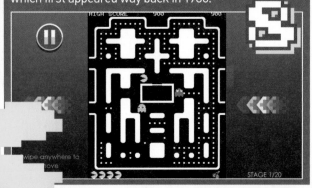

Retro games work really well on mobile devices, and this one is always worth revisiting. Move PAC-MAN around the mazes, collecting pills, and eating ghosts, as you attempt to rack up a high score. This pack includes numerous themed mazes to add a much-needed degree of variety to the game, which first appeared way back in 1980.

SKY FORCE 2014

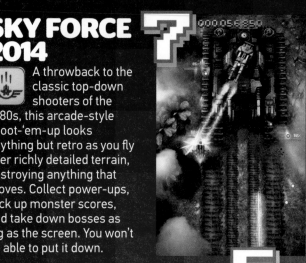

A throwback to the classic top-down shooters of the 1980s, this arcade-style shoot-'em-up looks anything but retro as you fly over richly detailed terrain, destroying anything that moves. Collect power-ups, rack up monster scores, and take down bosses as big as the screen. You won't be able to put it down.

7

DOODLE JUMP

This game has the simple aim of getting as high as possible. You jump up the various platforms, evading the many perils in your way to gain as much height as you can. You can collect bonuses, such as jetpacks, to ease your journey and experience a variety of themed worlds. Place your height marker and invite your friends to beat it.

5

CUT THE ROPE: MAGIC

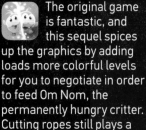

The original game is fantastic, and this sequel spices up the graphics by adding loads more colorful levels for you to negotiate in order to feed Om Nom, the permanently hungry critter. Cutting ropes still plays a huge part in the proceedings, but now you can also employ magic to help you deliver the candy to its salivating destination.

6

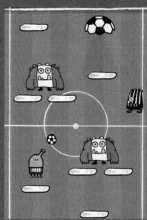

EXPERT COMMENT RYAN BUTT

Former Editor of *Apps Magazine*

With mobile gaming platforms taken as seriously, if not more so, than regular games consoles, we're blessed with an incredible variety of great games to pick up and play. Thousands more are released every week. But however complex the gameplay grows, and however astounding the graphics get, often simplicity shines brightest. This is evident from games like *Angry Birds* and the brilliant *Plants vs Zombies* riding high in this collection of the greatest mobile games ever.

The best games are often incredibly easy to pick up and play, equally appealing to men, women, and children. And don't be fooled into thinking that the latest in a series of games is the best. Often the original games that first burst onto the scene and captivated us are those that better stand the test of time. So with mobile games being significantly cheaper than—yet just as deep as—their console counterparts, your mobile device is surely your go-to for all things gaming.

MINECRAFT: POCKET EDITION

If you just don't want to stop playing *Minecraft*, now you can take it with you wherever you go. The game is just as fun on mobile, and a new feature called "Minecraft Realms" lets you play with your friends, no matter what device they're using. Work together (or against each other), as you explore the lands and defeat enemies.

PLAGUE INC.

A strategy game with a difference—the aim being to destroy the human race rather than save it—*Plague Inc.* features simple touchscreen controls to help you plot the destruction of the world by spreading diseases. Don't think that humankind is going to go quietly, though. You will have to work hard to take down the defenses and pollute each continent, country by country.

SPACE MARSHALS

Sci-fi meets Wild West in this tactical top-down shooter, as you pursue the galaxy's deadliest outlaws. Use the environment to pick off each outlaw's sharpshooting henchmen before apprehending the big bosses. The locations are varied, exciting, and littered with cool new firepower to aid your intergalactic fight for justice.

1 PLANTS VS. ZOMBIES

This is the ultimate tower defense game, combining frantic gameplay with gut-busting humor. With the zombie apocalypse in full swing, and the zombie hordes shuffling toward your front door, you need to set up plant-based installations to keep them at bay. Using balls of Sun as currency to purchase turrets, you have to ensure that your defenses outgun the increasing number of zombies and unlock new types of turrets to use against the bigger, more determined enemies. There are loads of extras to unlock and plenty of replay value. The sequel is also well worth checking out, but nothing comes close to the charm of the original.

A BLUETOOTH CONTROLLER

Controllers like the SteelSeries Nimbus are great for those with little experience in mobile gaming. They're comfortable to hold during long sessions, and often include pressure-sensitive buttons that have different functions depending on how hard you press. Most are wireless, with built-in batteries, and they're usually designed to work with iPhones and Android, so you can use them on some of the best mobile games around, including *Minecraft*, *Real Racing*, and *Lumino City*.

BEST MOBILE-GAMING ACCESSORIES

GAMING ACCESSORIES YOU SIMPLY NEED TO OWN

You don't need to own a console to have a great gaming experience. Smartphones are capable of running fantastic games, and there are thousands to download. But to get the best mobile-gaming experience, you may want accessories. Headsets, controllers, and keyboards aren't just for console and PC gamers; some are built especially for mobiles. Check out a few of these products, and your mobile experience will never be the same.

A WIRELESS MOUSE

If you're a fan of FPS games, a wireless mouse can improve your accuracy. Accessories such as Microsoft's Mobile Mouse connect to your Android smartphone, and include all of the basic functions you'd expect from a PC mouse, such as scroll wheels.

A MOBILE CONSOLE

Devices like the Mad Catz M.O.J.O. are full consoles, packed with great mobile games. They connect to your TV and can be used with lots of different controllers. If you want great smartphone games on the big screen, devices like these provide the best of both worlds.

A VR HEADSET

Do you want to play some virtual reality games on your smartphone? Then you need to check out an accessory like Homido VR. All you do is slide your smartphone in to the front and you'll be able to play some of the best VR games around, like *Bamf VR* and *Radial-G: Infinity*.

PHONE CASE CONTROLLER

Special cases, like Flitch.io, can add gaming controls to your smartphone. Make sure you get a model that's compatible with your smartphone, then snap your phone into the case. Joysticks on the back can be controlled with your middle fingers when holding your smartphone sideways. Plus, with shoulder buttons on the top, you'll get an extra level of control.

>BEST MOBILE-GAMING ACCESSORIES

CONTROLLER ADD-ON

Turning your iPhone into a full gaming controller is easy with devices like the Logitech PowerShell. These controllers have full console controls, including shoulder buttons, to give you an advantage when playing against your friends online, or even just in single-player.

SURROUND-SOUND HEADPHONES

If you want to make your mobile gaming feel more epic, the best way to do it is with a set of mobile-gaming headphones with surround- sound. Grab a pair of with cushioned ear pads, like the M Sevens from Turtle Beach, so that they're comfortable to wear, too.

ON-SCREEN JOYSTICK

Joysticks can give you the edge when you're gaming, so accessories like the ScreenStick are useful pieces of equipment. They stick right to your mobile's display, providing a joystick that's really durable. It will feel like you're playing on an old-school arcade machine!

GAMING KEYBOARDS

Devices like the MadCatz S.T.R.I.K.E. keyboard are ideal for those who want a PC-style gaming experience on their mobile device. They offer full keyboards, and the keys are often programmable to any functions you want. Some even include a mouse pad for extra control over your games, just in case you don't have a wireless mouse.

MULTIPLAYER GAMING HEADSET

If you're serious about mobile gaming, then a multiplayer headset—featuring a microphone so you can chat to your friends—can be great. Headsets like the Razer Kraken Mobile offer enough power to really improve your gaming experience, but are lightweight enough to make transporting them easy. High-quality speakers deliver amazing sound, so no matter what you're playing, you'll be blown away. Plus, you'll often find built-in media controls, via buttons on the cable. These allow you to adjust your phone's audio, if the game or chat become a little too loud for your liking.

DOTS & CO

CHARMING, RELAXING, AND LOVEABLE

Plenty of mobile games keep you busy during downtime, but there aren't many that help you to chill. That's why we love *Dots & Co*. It challenges your mind, but in a calm and relaxing way. The concept is simple enough: move through a series of levels, each with their own escalating challenge, and match dots together in a sequence. It holds your attention by shifting the structure throughout; you face various challenges, such as clearing a certain number of each color or clearing obstacles from the board, before you can progress. It's a lot of fun and that rare type of experience that's as charming as it is calming—just be prepared to wait for your charge to build back up again when you run out.

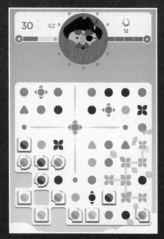

Although the game looks simple, it's beautifully crafted and has a great audio accompaniment.

Dots & Co takes a simple matching mechanic and builds a unique game around it. Making squares will remove all the dots of that color, which is usually the key to completing a level.

> ALSO CHECK OUT

Two Dots

SIMPLY CONNECT DOTS

The predecessor to *Dots & Co*, *Two Dots* is a simplified version of the same concept. What it lacks in structure, it makes up for in highly replayable fun. Simply connect dots.

Dots: A Game About Connecting

Do you just want to connect dots without the distraction of storylines, companions, or any other nonsense? Then, get your hands on *Dots*. Not only is it free, it's surprisingly challenging.

TIPS & TRICKS

≡ SEEK BIG POINTS
For a quick route to success, draw squares or rectangles. You'll clear all the other dots of the same color.

≡ BE SPEEDY
The faster you can match the colors in a round, the better your potential score will be.

≡ USE FRIENDS' POWERS
Choose a companion that has a useful power, and trigger them by clearing the triangle dots. They can turn the tide!

Learn to slide round the corners to get the maximum acceleration out of the bend.

stats

Featuring
140 DETAILED VEHICLES

Enjoy a total of
60 PLAYABLE EVENTS

17 REAL-WORLD LOCATIONS
to navigate

≣ RECKLESS RACING 3

DIRTIER, CRAZIER, AND FASTER THAN EVER

Reckless Racing returns for its third lap of the mobile track, pushing the limit with a huge selection of new vehicles, tracks, and events to haphazardly cruise through. All with the swipe of a finger. While it starts a little slowly—sticking you with a Class-C buggy—it only gets more fun. You build up a selection of powerful cars and trucks in your garage by winning races, nailing drift courses, and smashing the precision stunt-driving mode, "Gymkhana."

> **ALSO CHECK OUT**

Asphalt 8: Airborne

 Asphalt is one of the longest-lasting racing franchises available on mobile—probably because it's such a joy to play. With blazing speeds and great on-track action, *Asphalt* offers a comprehensive racing package.

Real Racing 3

 Real Racing 3 is generally considered to be the closest to a console-grade racing game you can find on a mobile device. It requires attention and finesse, but its stunning graphics and options make it a "must-play."

TIPS & TRICKS

≣ **WATCH THE ROAD**
While the idea is to be reckless, you need to stay on the track. Look out for tough scenery and adjust your drift accordingly.

≣ **FLEX YOUR WEIGHT**
Crash into the back of a heavier car that's dominating the road to make it tailspin out of the way.

≣ **CAMERA CONTROL**
In Settings, activate a "Chase Camera." This gives you a clearer view of the road ahead—great for anticipating corners.

BEST PUZZLE GAMES

INTRODUCING SOME TRIPLE-A HEAD-SCRATCHERS

The puzzle genre is one of the most popular on mobile devices, since games can be picked up and played by anyone, anywhere. A lot of the puzzle games featured here focus on matching up multiple items within a game board to score points, but there are also more original brainteasers to test your gray matter, too. Best of all, many of these games can be played for free!

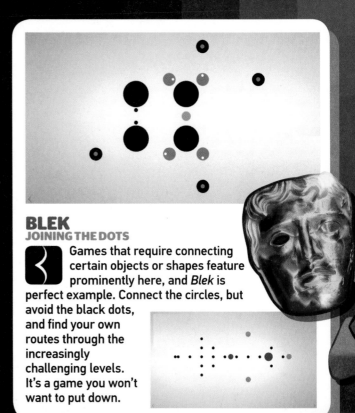

BLEK
JOINING THE DOTS

Games that require connecting certain objects or shapes feature prominently here, and *Blek* is perfect example. Connect the circles, but avoid the black dots, and find your own routes through the increasingly challenging levels. It's a game you won't want to put down.

LARA CROFT GO
TOMB TIME

Anyone who has ever played one of the many *Tomb Raider* games will know all about Lara Croft and her treasure-plundering exploits. This app takes inspiration from those games and shifts the action to a more puzzle-oriented domain. Each level is set to a game board and you, as Lara, have to move around, one space at a time, to overcome obstacles, deadly traps, and enemies. It works very well and manages to capture the spirit of the series, while making it easy to play on the move.

CUT THE ROPE
FEED THE BEAST

It seems like a simple task: get the candy into the monster's mouth. But *Cut the Rope* requires you to swipe the ropes suspending the candy and guide it past various pitfalls in order to feed the creature. Moving the candy through bonus stars will enhance your score and new hazards soon come into play to make life harder. With over 400 levels, this is no cakewalk, but the way in which the challenge is steadily ramped up, plus bags of charm, make this a great game.

FRAMED
COMPLETE THE COMICS

This original puzzle game has you switching panels in a comic strip to progress and finish the story. Some stylish graphics drive the theme and the action is accompanied by a slick, jazzy soundtrack. On the hunt for something different? This is it.

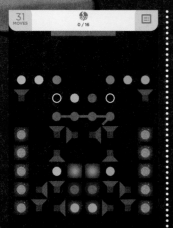

BEST FIENDS
THE ULTIMATE BUG REPELLENT

Not to be confused with the many match-up games available, *Best Fiends* provides a good balance of mental workout and enjoyment. It allows you to make diagonal moves on the game board as you string together leaves, dew drops, and mushrooms.

level 12 5x5

flows: 4/5   moves: 4   best: -   pipe: 95%

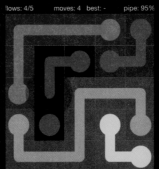

3 x ?

WHERE'S MY WATER?
WATER CARRY ON!

Help Swampy the alligator get water to his shower by cutting a path through the dirt. Guide the stream of liquid past various hazards and collectibles before channeling it down the pipe to its destination. The full version has over 500 challenges to overcome.

TWO DOTS
MORE COLOR CONNECTING

Often, the key to a great puzzle game is simplicity, and they don't come much simpler than *Two Dots*. The aim is to join up clusters of same-colored dots to hit number targets, and you get monster points for connecting in squares. It's lots of fun but be warned—it gets hard very quickly.

FLOW FREE
GO WITH THE FLOW

A prime example of a simple, hard-to-put-down puzzle game, the aim is to connect the dots without crossing the lines. Every square on the screen must be used, and more dots come into play with every batch of levels. This game is simple fun for gaming on the go.

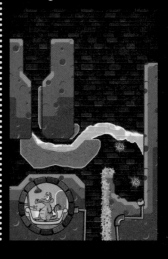

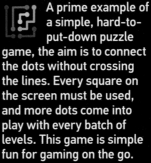

Always be aware of how gravity impacts the level, or you'll end up getting squished by big, spiky blocks.

:STATS

3 LIVES PER LEVEL
in the free-to-play version

40 LEVELS
to roll through

360: Rotate each stage
360 GAMES

> ## ALSO CHECK OUT

Silly Sausage in Meat Land
 It's another game about avoiding hazards, but this time you control a dog that can stretch like Mr. Fantastic.

INKS
 This is a cool pinball game where you pick up colors as you flick your ball around the table, making a painting at the same time as you play the game.

BENEATH THE LIGHTHOUSE
A BEACON OF BRILLIANCE

We can't help but feel sorry for the main character in this great little puzzle game—he spends all his time tumbling down tunnels! Still, that will only make you more determined to guide him to safety. Each of the game's circular rooms can be spun 360 degrees, sending your character rolling around the walls like a ball as you change which way is up or down. You've got to use quick reactions to spin the room back and forth, avoiding hazards as you guide your character to the exit.

≡ TAKE YOUR TIME
Rushing is sure to end in failure. Go slow the first time around, and come back later for the gold medal.

≡ CLEAR YOUR PATH
Sometimes, getting to the end isn't all you have to worry about. Look out for obstacles that you have to move.

≡ WATCH FOR BOMBS
Bombs that explode on contact are one of the trickiest things to deal with. Plan a route that rolls them away from you.

TRUE SKATE

EXTREME FUN

You know those miniature skateboards you can get that you control with your fingers? Well, imagine if you could take those into a real skatepark and you've got yourself *True Skate*. The board appears on screen without a rider and you push, ollie, and flip it with flicks of your fingers.

The touch controls are really intuitive—rather than worrying about complicated button combos, you just turn and flick the board with your fingers as you would with your feet in real life. There are missions for you to try and complete if you want, but it is fun just to play around in the park, too. Once you have mastered the extensive array of tricks, you can have great fun stringing them together in fluid runs for massive points.

CROOKED GRIND
Score: 378

Flipping in and out of a grind and landing the combo feels amazing. Be sure to mix up your tricks for big scores though

Landing the more complicated tricks can be really difficult, as often the board may land on its side, or upside down. Keep practising and you'll soon learn that timing is everything.

› ALSO CHECK OUT

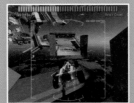

Jet Car Stunts 2
If pulling off tricks is your thing then check out another title from *True Skate* developer True Axis. Nailing cool stunts in a versatile jet-propelled car is the name of the game here.

Joe Danger
Step into the shoes of a stuntman to jump off ramps, leap over shark tanks, and avoid traps on your trusty motorcycle. The game has leaderboards, so you can compete to get the best scores with your friends.

TIPS & TRICKS

▤ DON'T SKIP THE TUTORIAL
It takes a while to get the hang of *True Skate* so we recommend getting the basics down before you jump in.

▤ USE THE REPLAY
It's worth knowing the game has a great replay function that you can use to rewatch your most spectacular tricks.

▤ EXPERIMENT
You're not punished for failing in *True Skate*, so just spend some time having fun to see what's possible.

SHOWCASE
LUMINO CITY

Lumino City tempts you in almost as soon as you set eyes on its cute characters and colorful buildings. There's a mystery to solve and an astonishing handcrafted world to explore laid out in front of you. It's got fantastic puzzles designed specifically for a touchscreen, making it one of the best adventure games on mobile devices.

This is your introduction to *Lumino City*. The puzzles can be pretty odd at times—the first one involves fixing an electrical circuit using lemons!

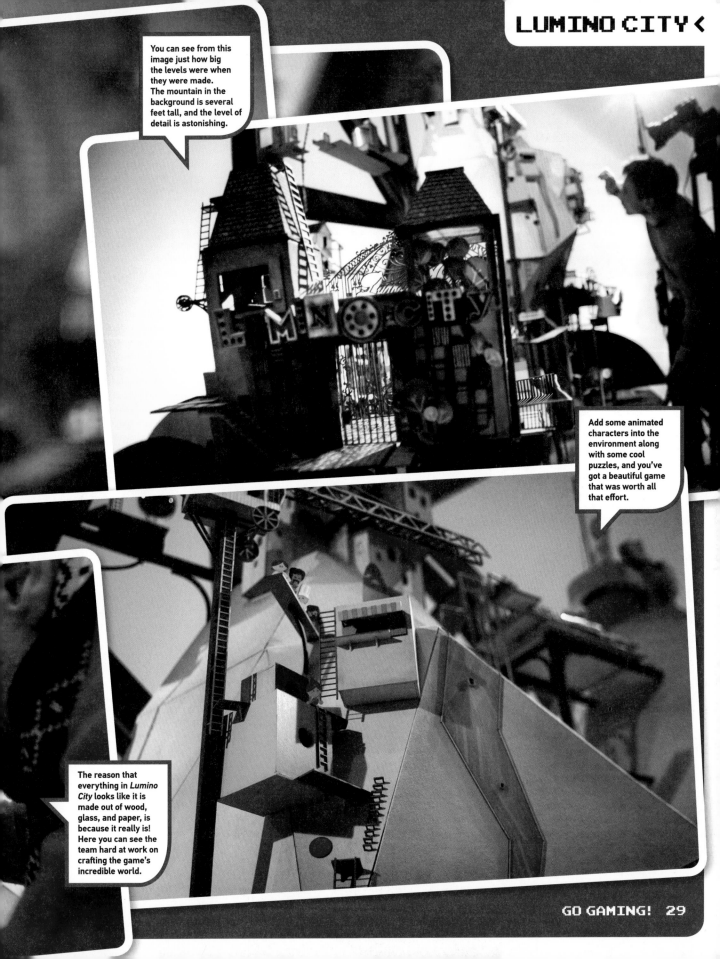

You can see from this image just how big the levels were when they were made. The mountain in the background is several feet tall, and the level of detail is astonishing.

Add some animated characters into the environment along with some cool puzzles, and you've got a beautiful game that was worth all that effort.

The reason that everything in *Lumino City* looks like it is made out of wood, glass, and paper, is because it really is! Here you can see the team hard at work on crafting the game's incredible world.

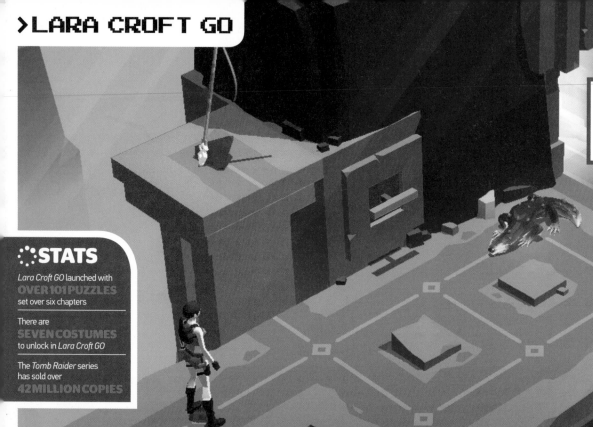

These lizards will chase you down once they spot you, but we've spotted a spear that might come in handy!

STATS

Lara Croft GO launched with **OVER 101 PUZZLES** set over six chapters

There are **SEVEN COSTUMES** to unlock in *Lara Croft GO*

The *Tomb Raider* series has sold over **42 MILLION COPIES**

LARA CROFT GO
A REAL TREASURE

Imagine *Tomb Raider* as a board game, and you're halfway to *Lara Croft GO*. The game takes the key elements of the *Tomb Raider* series—puzzle solving, treasure hunting, climbing, and combat—but uses them in their simplest form. In each of the game's beautiful, minimalist stages, you can move Lara one space at a time. Enemies also move, meaning you have to plan ahead to grab the treasure you want without getting trapped! This game is guaranteed to test your brain.

ALSO CHECK OUT

Hitman GO
Hitman GO is very similar to *Lara Croft GO*, with characters being represented by pieces in board game world. Your job is to reach your target, then get out without being caught!

Monument Valley
If you love the minimalist art style and turn-based puzzle solving of *Lara Croft GO*, then you would definitely find *Monument Valley* a lot of fun.

TREASURE HUNT
Take the time to explore each stage. There are relics hidden throughout *Lara Croft's GO*'s levels.

THINK FIRST
There's no time pressure in this game, so take it slow and plan a few moves ahead.

TARGETS ACQUIRED
You don't only have to use spears on enemies. They can be used to trigger traps and levers, too!

≣ POCKET LEAGUE STORY 2

MANAGE YOUR WAY TO SOCCER GREATNESS

Take control of a new soccer team in *Pocket League 2*. Build it up from a group of amateurs into an all-conquering force, using training, tactics, player transfers, sponsorship deals, and a whole lot more. Being able to manage every single aspect of your club and then seeing all your hard work pay off in results make this game hard to put down.

You'll start to form connections with your players as they develop. But be warned, you might start to love these little guys even more than the real-life stars of your favorite soccer team!

⟨⟩ STATS

32 ACHIEVEMENTS
to unlock

14 UPGRADEABLE
soccer facilities

8 LEAGUES
to conquer

Your club won't look all that spectacular at the start. However, once you start upgrading your facilities, things will quickly get a lot more impressive!

Some players perform better on different surfaces. It's worth paying attention to where your next game is and changing your team if necessary.

⟩ ALSO CHECK OUT

New Star Soccer

Instead of taking charge of a whole team, *New Star Soccer* has you take control of one player's career. Unlike *Pocket League 2*, you also get to take part in the action.

Football Manager Mobile 2016

For a more realistic soccer management sim with both real players and clubs, you need to check out the mobile version of the legendary *Football Manager* series.

TIPS & TRICKS

≣ EXCEPTIONAL TALENT

If you see a player labeled as "Exceptional", try picking them up—they will develop their skills faster than other players.

≣ BRING IN THE CASH

Don't spend all your cash on players. Upgrade your facilities and you'll generate more money to spend.

≣ EQUIP ITEMS

Make sure you don't forget to equip unlocked items so that your players get the benefits.

MINECRAFT: POCKET EDITION

MARVELOUS MOBILE MINING

Thanks to this ore-some mobile version of the world's most popular game, you can now mine, build, and craft—no matter where you are. You can do almost anything in *Minecraft*, from building a huge castle complete with drawbridge to creating a working computer using Redstone. Of course, if you just want to start a farm, you can do that, too.

The coolest thing about the mobile version, though, is the ability to jump into online games with your friends using the new "Minecraft Realms" service, no matter what kind of device they're using. So you can play with friends using the *Pocket Edition* or Windows 10 versions of the game, and play together to create a world of your own, or create multiplayer modes that see you facing off to become a champion!

> ## ALSO CHECK OUT

Terraria

 Like *Minecraft*, *Terraria* is an exploration game, and is available on pretty much every platform. The randomly generated worlds are stuffed with everything you need for great crafting adventures.

Block Fortress

 Block Fortress is all about surviving hordes of bad guys intent on overwhelming your fortresses. Mine valuable resources to build a (hopefully) impenetrable barracks and mighty weapons to keep those unwanted visitors out.

TIPS & TRICKS

≡ STARTING OUT?
First things first—you need to make a bed to sleep in, find some food, and make some tools to get crafting.

≡ TRASH IT
Place a cactus on any sandy area, pop on a trapdoor, and you've created a trash can.

≡ CRACK FOR A COMPASS
If you whack a block—taking care not to smash it—the directions of the cracks will tell you which way is north, south, east, and west.

TOP 5 ITEMS

You can jump into third-person mode to see your character from behind in the menu of *Minecraft: Pocket Edition*.

PICKAXE

Doubling as both a useful tool and an excellent weapon, the pickaxe really is a must-have item. It also enables you to dig down beneath the surface of the world and find more valuable resources in caves—which is kind of essential in a game called *Minecraft*.

CHESTS

There are lots of useful things to pick up in *Minecraft*. But what do you do if you spot something you want, but your inventory is already full? You need extra storage! Pick up any chests you find in mines, or craft your own from wood, to store all of your items.

DIAMONDS

Diamonds are one of the toughest materials to mine in *Minecraft*, but finding them is essential if you want to be a powerful player. Collect enough and you can create the toughest weapons and armor, which is vital if you decide to take on bosses like the Ender Dragon.

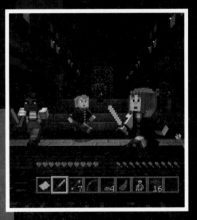

TORCHES

Sometimes, the simple things are the most valuable. Craft torches using a piece of coal and a wooden stick and you'll be able to light your way through dark caves, or brighten up your home. If it's too dark, monsters will start to spawn, so watch out!

WOOD

Wood is probably the most important resource in *Minecraft*. Thankfully, the stuff is everywhere! You'll need wood to make tools and torches, so keeping a good supply of it is a really good idea in case you suddenly run out of light as night falls.

BEST TOTALLY UNIQUE MOBILE GAMES

UNLIKE ANYTHING YOU'VE PLAYED BEFORE!

Mobile devices allow developers to make games that wouldn't be possible anywhere else. Crazy motion controls, weird story lines and simple touchscreen interfaces help set titles like these apart from the rest of the games on the app store. If you're looking for something a little bit different from your gaming, these are the games to bring it.

THE BANNER SAGA

This stunning hand-drawn 2-D game is inspired by Norse mythology and presents a tale where every story, and every decision, is a matter of life and death. If you've got a sturdy composition and a willingness to stick with your squad, no matter what, you won't be disappointed.

ROLLERCOASTER TYCOON

Before *The Sims* and *Goat Simulator*, there was *RollerCoaster Tycoon*, one of gaming's very first management simulation games. The mobile version brings all 18 scenarios from the original game, a fantastic sandbox mode, five park themes, dynamic weather, and no in-app purchases. You can even ride the rides!

VVVVVV

Nope, that's not a typo. *VVVVVV* is a polished puzzle platformer with a twist: instead of jumping, you flip gravity to help you maneuver around obstacles in search of your missing crew. It is fun, funny, and furiously tricky in places, but you really can't go wrong with this retro-inspired game. It's unique and you won't be able to put it down.

MONUMENT VALLEY

 Monument Valley is not only stunning, it's also one of the best puzzlers we've ever played on mobile (or otherwise). Guiding princess Ida through these gorgeous—if geometrically impossible—architectural masterpieces rarely feels like a chore, even when tackling those point-and-click puzzles!

NUB'S ADVENTURE

 Nub's Adventure may look like any other old-school platformer. However, here is a game stuffed with secrets if you're prepared to jump off the beaten path and explore a little. With loads of different perks, the game rarely feels stale, even when you're several hours in.

PRUNE

Everything happens in real time in *Prune*. With each trim and chop, you must nurture your trees to help them grow strong and flower despite the environment or weather conditions. Chopping down trees has never been so serene as it is in *Prune*.

GRIM FANDANGO REMASTERED

If you have yet to play *Grim Fandango*, we must introduce you to Manny Calavera, the world's weirdest travel agent. There's a reason people often refer to the game as one of the great point-and-click adventure games ever made, you know. Just play it and you'll see why, too!

SNOWBOARD PARTY 2

With *Snowboard Party 2*, you can show off on the slopes any time of year, in any weather! A classic 3-D sports game, it's full of loads of modes and styles. You can even pull in your own tunes while you grind those rails!

GOAT SIMULATOR

It seems like a joke, we know, but *Goat Simulator* not only exists, there's now a mobile version! So if you've ever wondered what it's like to be a goat (and who hasn't, really?), *Goat Simulator* is here to give you the chance to experience the ups and downs of life as a goat …

FRAMED

If you like to think of yourself as an armchair detective, why not give the beautifully designed puzzler *Framed* a try? In this game, you must rearrange the panels of an animated comic book to change the outcome of the story. Can you change events for the better? Or will you make everything worse?

RIDICULOUS FISHING

Bright, bold, and a little bewildering, *Ridiculous Fishing* starts off as you'd expect: a guy in a boat with a fishing pole. But as you progress, our fisherman becomes more and more impatient, eventually taking aquatic spoils out with guns and bazookas. We love it!

DOWNWELL

Downwell delivers exactly what it says in the title. Tumbling down a never-ending well, your job is to survive each bump and crash, as well as the objects falling on your head, too. Oh, and did we mention the hero's boots are guns? Fire those bad boys!

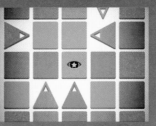

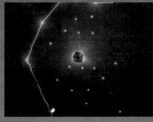

SWAPPEROO

Swapperoo requires you to match and eradicate lines of matching tiles. What's different here, however, is that the tiles can only move in certain directions, and you need to spend time learning special moves and tricks to chain your moves.

BEYONDIUM

You need quick thinking and quick fingers for this game! In *Beyondium* you must connect dots of the same color with lines to destroy the particles. Link to the wrong color, however, and you'll have to start over. It's easier said than done!

DOCTOR WHO: LEGACY

Though based upon the popular match-three puzzle style, *Doctor Who: Legacy*—a mobile game officially licensed by the BBC—draws heavily on *Doctor Who* lore, bringing a whole new dimension to these type of puzzlers. Stuffed with every character you can think of—including very new ones!—this is a must for every *Who* fan.

No energy meters, No tricks!

ASPHALT 8: AIRBORNE

We've picked the eighth edition of this game but in truth, all of the *Asphalt* games are pretty fantastic. With hours of gameplay packed into several modes—including multiplayer—*Asphalt 8* is just as fun as it looks, with awesome graphics and gripping music. It's time to hit the road!

THE BEGGAR'S RIDE

Anyone who says you can't get great graphics on a mobile device and even greater storytelling hasn't tried *The Beggar's Ride*. Stuffed with clever puzzles, this platformer sees you start off as a lowly beggar who, by collecting mysterious masks, sees the world through the eyes of an all-powerful being.

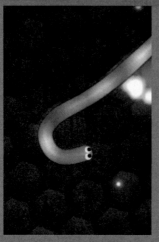

SLITHER.IO

Despite its deceptively simplistic appearance, *slither.io* is one of the world's biggest—and best—massively multiplayer games to play online. It's super-slithery fun to play alone or with your buddies, and is available as both a mobile and browser game, so you can slither around whenever you want!

MINECRAFT: POCKET EDITION

There have been many games trying to emulate its success, but when it comes to unique gaming, you need to go back to the original and best—*Minecraft: Pocket Edition*! The touchscreen controls work great on this mobile version, and you can play with friends online in the new *Realms* mode.

EXPERT COMMENT
LAURA K. DALE
Video Games Critic

Pokémon GO has had a huge effect on the way social mobile gaming brings friends together, and is seen by the general public.

It uses the GPS data in your phone, with real-world location data, to drop the original Pokémon into the world around you. There could be a Porygon at the bus stop, or a Pikachu down by the pier. The only way to find them is to get out into the world exploring.

The social aspects of the game, which encourage friends to meet up with each other, as well as the addition of a vibrant layer of mystery and intrigue to a normally mundane world, make *Pokémon GO* a great way to play with friends, and spice up every day life.

POKÉMON GO

Catching Pokémon in the real world has been a dream of gamers for a long time. Now, thanks to some clever augmented reality technology and this cool app, you can finally live that dream. Pokémon like Pikachu and Jigglypuff appear on a map that shows the area around you. All you need to do is go to that spot and you can capture them using Poké Balls. Once you've got a powerful team of Pokémon, you can take on a local Gym to become the leader and claim your reward of coins!

If your data package allows it, make sure you take your phone with you on vacation . . . Pokémon vary by region, so if you're visiting friends or family, keep your Poké Balls ready.

> **"ONCE YOU'VE GOT A POWERFUL TEAM, YOU CAN TAKE ON A LOCAL GYM."**

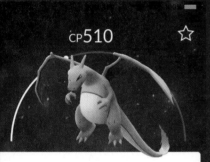

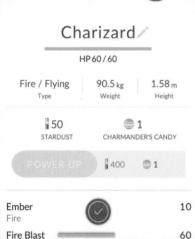

Each Pokémon has unique stats, such as their CP (combat power) and HP (hit points.) You can increase these stats by spending Stardust and Candy to power up your Pokémon. If you have enough Candy, you can even evolve your Pokémon into a new form, with more powerful stats and attacks.

CP510

☆

Charizard ✎

HP 60 / 60

Fire / Flying	90.5 kg	1.58 m
Type	Weight	Height

🔹50
STARDUST

🔴1
CHARMANDER'S CANDY

POWER UP   🔹400   🔴1

Ember		10
Fire	✓	
Fire Blast		60

Vixxiie

Lumino City is a fantastic game to escape into, and there is much to explore within the unique landscapes you travel through.

STATS

$868
daily revenue estimate

174
daily installs

3
BAFTA award nominations

> ALSO
CHECK OUT

Kiwanuka
This puzzle action game requires you to guide tiny citizens to freedom, instructing them to build towers, grab ledges, and form bridges. Careful thought and timing is required.

Trick Shot
The aim of the game is to throw a ball into a box—which sounds easy, right? Wrong! You have to arrange objects and get the angles just right to land the ball successfully.

LUMINO CITY
A PUZZLE ADVENTURE WITH A DIFFERENCE

As puzzle adventures go, this one stands out because of its ultracool environments. They have been handcrafted out of everyday objects to create unique locations and backdrops. As Lumi, you have to track down your missing grandfather. To find him you have to explore the city and figure out the various mechanisms that power the world. Only then can you break free from its confines and get one step closer to your missing relative. With superb graphics, this game presents a tough but beautiful challenge that will live long in your memory.

TIPS & TRICKS

CONQUER THE STAIRS
To clear the stairs just after Grandad's house, pick up the stick from the ground and use it to ring the bell just up to the left.

TAP EVERYTHING
You'll need to explore every corner of the world to beat the game, so tap everywhere!

ASK FOR HELP
Some puzzles might seem impossible to you, but a friend might see the solution instantly.

MONUMENT VALLEY

THE EIGHTH WONDER OF THE WORLD

The mind-bending brilliance of *Monument Valley* has made it one of the biggest hits in mobile games. The puzzle game uses perspective in really clever ways, allowing you to spin, flip, and rotate parts of the world to open up new paths for the princess you are controlling. Optical illusions and crazy geometry are used to create some really smart puzzles that often surprise you when they reveal something you couldn't see before. That great gameplay is supported by fantastic audio and an amazing visual style that makes every screen look like a painting.

:::STATS

Monument Valley has been installed on over
10 MILLION SEPARATE DEVICES

AROUND 50%
of players who started *Monument Valley* completed it

It took eight team members
55 WEEKS
to make *Monument Valley*

That big crank in the middle of the stage is a pretty big clue about what you need to do here!

›ALSO CHECK OUT

Wonderputt

The floating world and weird geometrical logic of this crazy golf game are very similar to *Monument Valley*. We love the way new holes appear as you play.

Superbrothers: Sword & Sworcery EP

This game has been cited as an inspiration for *Monument Valley* by the game's developers. Why not give it a try yourself and see if you can spot any of the similarities?

TIPS & TRICKS

≡ TAP EVERYTHING
Start each level by playing around with all its different parts and seeing what you can do.

≡ GET RID OF CROWS
If a crow is getting in your way, there's usually a platform you can raise, lower, or rotate to move them somewhere else.

≡ NEVER FEAR
It's impossible to get yourself stuck in a situation you can't get out of, so feel free to experiment.

There are a variety of huge bosses to be discovered and battled by intrepid explorers. You better have some good weapons at the ready, though.

STATS

OVER 100 MPH
max possible speed

17+ MILLIONS
sales to date

OVER 3,000
items including weapons and armor

TERRARIA
CRAFTING YOUR OWN FUN

Some games can struggle when they make the move from console or PC to mobile, but not *Terraria*. The developer has done a fantastic job of making the game work with touch controls. This means you can now take the game's huge procedurally generated worlds wherever you go, exploring caves, mining for resources, crafting new tools, fighting monsters, and more in this brilliant world-builder. You can see why people often describe this title as a 2-D *Minecraft*, but give the game a try, and you'll soon discover that there is far more to it than that.

> ## ALSO CHECK OUT

Minecraft: Pocket Edition
If you want more of that adventure and freedom that only procedurally generated games can offer by giving you unique worlds to explore that you can change in any way you want, but want it all in 3-D, then *Minecraft* is for you.

Crashlands
If you love the elements of survival and crafting in *Terraria*, you are sure to enjoy *Crashlands*, a game in which you have to survive on an alien planet teeming with hostile life.

TIPS & TRICKS

BUILD THE BACK
Don't forget to build the back wall! Without it, monsters can still get in to your 2-D buildings.

TRENCHTOWN
Building a trench on either side of your house is a great way to protect it from attacks.

TIME TO TINKER
Once you have defeated a Goblin Army, explore the caverns to find the Goblin Tinkerer, who will sell you useful items.

SKYLANDERS SUPERCHARGERS

PUT THE PEDAL TO THE METAL

The cool thing about the *Skylanders* series is that it lets you take real-life collectible figures and transport them into the game world to play with. The advantage of the mobile version is that you can do that wherever you go, as long as you take your bluetooth Portal of Power along with you (don't worry, you can play with a free digital character if you don't have a Portal). That means you've got the freedom to enjoy *Skylanders SuperChargers'* blend of battling monsters, platforming, racing, and car combat wherever you go with your mobile device.

⟩ ALSO CHECK OUT

Skylanders Battlecast

For more *Skylanders* fun, check out *Battlecast*, a collectible card game where you build a deck of cards that you can level up on your way to defeating the evil Kaos.

LEGO Marvel Super Heroes: Universe in Peril

If you're looking for another action game with cool characters to play as, check out this LEGO Marvel game, where you can play as Hulk, Iron Man, Spider-Man, and many more famous superheroes.

⠿ STATS

OVER 240 MILLION
Skylanders toys have been sold worldwide

The biggest *Skylanders* collection consists of **4,100 SEPARATE ITEMS** and earned its owner a place in the *Guinness World Records*

In 2014, a group of skydivers played *Skylanders* at **12,500 FT. IN THE AIR**

The new racing and car combat sections that come with the introduction of vehicles work as well on the mobile version as the regular *Skylanders* gameplay.

TIPS & TRICKS

☰ HUNT FOR COLLECTIBLES
Keep an eye out for collectibles, which boost your characters' stats.

☰ UPGRADE VEHICLES
You can upgrade your vehicles with shields, weapons, and performance mods to make them more powerful.

☰ SWAP CHARACTERS
If your Skylander is taking a lot of damage, switch to another one so that they don't faint.

THE BEST FREE GAMES

FANTASTIC GAMES THAT DON'T COST A PENNY

Many great mobile games can be downloaded and played for free, which is great news if you're looking for something new and exciting to get stuck into. While it's true that many want you to purchase in-game currency to unlock content more quickly, there is absolutely no need to do so and you can continue to enjoy the games at no cost whatsoever. Here we round up some of the best free games. Make sure you check them out!

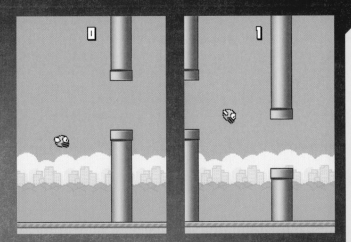

FLAPPY BIRD ORIGINAL VERSION

30

This game was a big hit a couple of years ago—and it is just as frustratingly tricky as ever. More so, in fact, because this version reverses the controls so that you have to tap the screen to go down instead of staying airborne. Your score is set by how many pipes you can swoop through.

RACING PENGUIN

28

This is a challenging physics-based slide-and-fly game in which you have to slide your penguin down the mountains of Antarctica. Build up speed and then flap your tiny wings to glide over gaps. The action takes place over five themed worlds with 40 levels to complete in all.

FOUR IN A ROW

29

Taking the classic *Connect Four* board game concept and applying it to a touchscreen interface, the aim of *Four in a Row* is simple. Place four counters of the same color in a row to win. Compete against other players from around the world and increase the challenge by upping the number of connected counters needed to win.

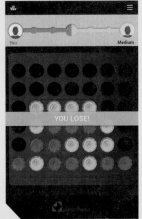

JENGA

27

Enjoy all the fun of the classic wooden tower game without having to pick up the pieces afterwards. Observe, examine, and remove loose blocks from the tower, and see how high you can get it before it topples. Classic retro fun for all the family.

THUMB DRIFT

26

Who doesn't love driving race cars around corners and performing tire-melting drifts? This game is all about the slides. Drift around tight bends, collect coins, and cover enough distance to get to the next stage. Awesome finger-sliding fun to get your heart racing.

KIM KARDASHIAN: HOLLYWOOD

25 In this surprisingly engrossing app, you get to live the Kardashian dream. You start by creating your own star and go on to deal with all of the pitfalls faced by popular reality stars. You will encounter pushy fans, decide what to wear on the all-important red carpet, and decorate your perfect house.

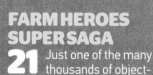
Feed Update!

Kim Kardashian @KimKardashian
Loving cruising around Hollywood in my BFF's new ride!
#BFFS #Hollywood

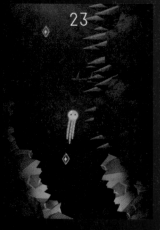

STEPS
23 The aim in *Steps* is to roll your cube along the path, tapping the screen at the right moment to pass various obstacles that pepper your route—all without being destroyed. It's a great game to dip into, and the challenge is soon ramped up to test your reflexes to the max.

SLIP AWAY
24 Tap either side of the screen to guide a small squid-like sea creature through underwater mazes, collecting bonuses along the way. Your creature requires constant guidance to evade enemies and obstacles. With awesome graphics and sound, this is well worth checking out.

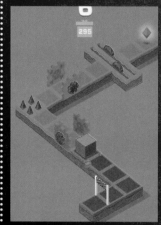

TOY BLAST
22 A fun and addictive matchup game. Tap on groups of the same colored blocks to clear them and hit your level targets, while freeing the toys within the board to wreak havoc and score massive bonuses. There are over 750 levels to complete, and you can play against your friends.

FARM HEROES SUPER SAGA
21 Just one of the many thousands of object-matching mobile games available, this one has you collecting "Cropsies" to stop Rancid Raccoon from ruining a country show. It sounds ridiculous, but with matchup fun as hard to put down as this, who cares?

GEOPETS

19 In this geolocation-based adventure, explore the real world in search of new creatures to capture, train, and battle against other players with. Using augmented reality, in-game graphics are layered onto photo images of the world around you for a truly immersive experience. It is a fun way to get in shape while exploring your surrounds.

SMASHY CITY

20 Picking one of many legendary monsters, you're let loose on a city to wreak as much havoc as possible. Stomp on skyscrapers, destroy entire estates, and take on the cops, SWAT teams, and armies that arrive on the scene to halt your rampaging. How much devastation can *you* cause?

SUPER STICKMAN GOLF 3

18 With challenging courses, power-ups, game modes, collectible cards, multiplayer matches, and loads of cool surprises, *Super Stickman Golf* isn't really a chill-out game. Can you master your swing and tame the somewhat bizarre courses by finding the quickest and easiest route to the hole?

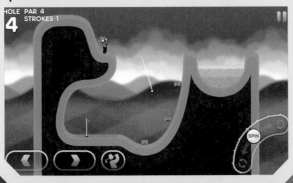

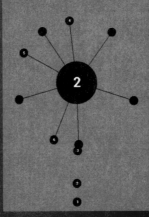

AA ARROW

17 A simple and enjoyable puzzle game, you are faced with a rotating circle with pins stuck in it. Tap to stick an additional bunch of pins into it without hitting any of the existing pins. Things soon get faster and gaps get smaller, testing your reflexes to the limit.

SMASH HIT

16 With hazards, obstacles, and barriers constantly speeding towards you, the aim is to smash through successfully by hurling ball bearings at them. You can tap anywhere on the screen to aim and launch your balls. There are also bonuses to earn and skillshots to pull off along the way.

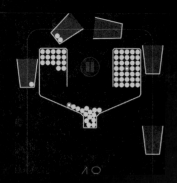

100 BALLS

15 With a selection of containers circling the screen, you have to tap to release balls from the pot as a container passes underneath to catch them. The balls will then be tipped back into the pot and the rotations will continue. Your game ends when you lose all of your balls or all of your containers. It's as simple, and frustrating, as that!

CLASH OF CLANS

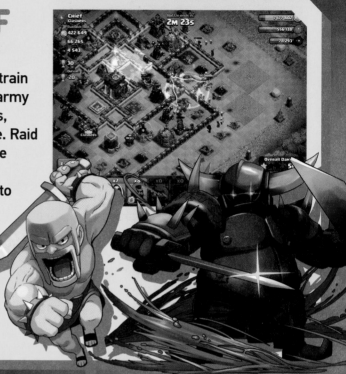

14 Raise and train your own army of warriors, then go on the rampage. Raid the camps of your online opponents and, in turn, repel all their attempts to pulverize and plunder your base. With loads of different troops and installations to unleash and use, it's the ultimate battle for supremacy.

BASKETBALL STARS

13 Lots of fun to play on your own, but even better for playing against online opponents, *Basketball Stars* is a street basketball game. The aim? Beat your opponents for cash. You can shoot baskets by swiping up and employing all manner of fancy footwork to outwit and outscore your opponents within the time limit. There are flashier clothes to unlock, increasingly more impressive courts to play on, and cool effects to keep you motivated when you're on a scoring streak.

SCORE! WORLD GOALS

12 Re-create some of history's greatest goals by passing, running into position, and slamming the ball into the net. It is like a puzzle game (complete with star ratings for level completion), but will appeal to soccer fans who just love scoring goals.

HILL CLIMB RACING

11 The challenge is to drive through the treacherous terrain littered with bumps, drips, and man-made obstacles. Clever use of the brake and accelerator is key to prevent your vehicle from flipping. The wacky car controls are tricky to get the hang of, but it's a lot of fun.

DUMB WAYS TO DIE

10

Packed with short, snappy mini-games, your aim is simple: complete whatever task is asked of you in any given level without dying in any one of hundreds of grisly ways. It could involve tilting your device or tapping the screen; either way its laugh-out-loud humor and variety make it a real mobile gaming classic.

Swat
TAP TO HIT THE WASPS

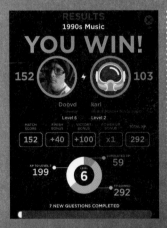

STICK HERO

8
A tricky reflex game, you use your ninja's stick to bridge the gap on each screen. You can "grow" your pole vertically by holding the screen, then dropping it to form a bridge. It does involve a little luck, though. If your bridge is too short or too long, you'll die. It's challenging, but fun.

QUIZUP

9
If you have a head full of information and no outlet for it, this app is for you. Compete against people from all over the world in a series of trivia questions in your choice of categories. You can build up the stats of your quiz profile over time, and even play on your own to build up your XP.

MOBILE STRIKE

7
Coming from the team that made the successful *Game of War*, *Mobile Strike* shares a lot of similarities. You must build a base, control the action, and test your troops on the battlefield to be successful. Join millions of online players to battle it out for global supremacy.

PAPER TOSS 2.0

6
Insanely enjoyable, this game—set in numerous locations around an office environment—requires you to flick paper balls into the trash can. You must contend with the breeze from a nearby fan, so get the angle just right to earn plenty of bonuses and unlock achievements.

> THE BEST FREE GAMES

NEED FOR SPEED NO LIMITS

5 The first edition of the long-running race series made just for mobile devices, *NFS No Limits* lets you build and customize your dream car. Next you take it on the road to compete in thrilling street races for cash and bragging rights. It drives fast and it looks absolutely amazing.

FIFA 16 ULTIMATE TEAM

4 Soccer fans will love the way the controls are simplified to bring all the silky skills and fluid play from the console versions of *FIFA* to mobile devices. Earn, trade, and transfer superstar players to create your own unbeatable dream team before you defeat your friends online.

MARVEL AVENGERS ACADEMY

3 Join your favorite superheroes in their college years and help them discover their super powers. With incredible comic book-style graphics, you complete missions to earn money, unlock XP, and build better facilities for your academy. A must for any Marvel fan.

HUNGRY SHARK WORLD

2 The sequel to the popular *Hungry Shark* game, this one includes more locations around the world. You roam the waters and survive by finding things to eat, such as smaller fish and bonus treasures. The graphics are dazzling and the increased variety in the levels means that it never gets boring.

GAMING!

ANGRY BIRDS 2

1 The official sequel to probably *the* most popular mobile game of all time, *Angry Birds 2* doesn't try to radically alter a winning formula. Instead it builds on the success of the first game by improving the graphics, adding in even more humor, and delivering a huge batch of fresh new levels for fans to tackle. The aim, as before, is to clear out all the pigs by catapulting as few birds as possible to amass as high a score as possible. It is just as much fun as ever.

EXPERT COMMENT

JACK PARSONS

EDITOR OF GADGET MAGAZINE

Angry Birds was the original must-have app for your mobile device. So simple that anyone could pick up and play, it also boasted surprising depth with clever puzzles and concealed bonus items that you would only pick up playing levels a second or third time around—okay, maybe even fourth, fifth, or sixth time around! But perhaps the main reason it was so popular, is that it was entirely free, so there was no barrier to everyone enjoying it.

This is why free games are so great. You can just download one, find out if you like it, and if not, delete it and try another one, like a buffet tablet of unlimited fun. The range of apps you can download at no cost is astounding. From puzzle games and racers, to adventure games and brain teasers, there's something for every taste. It's the ideal way to find out if you like a certain type of game, at no risk and at no cost.

Back in the lair, you choose the character, stage, and story, before jumping in and playing out your created scenario.

⚙ STATS

SIX
characters to unlock

100 STUDS
is enough to unlock your first lair item

0 COST:
DC Mighty Micros is free to play and has no in-app purchases

> ALSO CHECK OUT

LEGO Star Wars: The Complete Saga
This game combines the original *LEGO Star Wars* video game and the sequel, *LEGO Star Wars II: The Original Trilogy,* offering hours of fun!

LEGO City My City
This collection of mini-games, where you can do everything, from playing as an astronaut in space to exploring the deep sea, is ideal when you're on the go.

≣ LEGO DC MIGHTY MICROS

COMIC BOOK CHAOS

LEGO comes together with the DC Universe to create this cool mobile racer packed with superheroes and villains. In *Mighty Micros*, you build the scenarios you want to play by picking the hero, villain, setting, and so on, and then bringing it to life. As you chase down a villain in your vehicle—or escape from a hero, if you prefer—you can pick up collectibles. You can use those collectibles to unlock more characters and other component parts to build new stories, or unlock new areas in your lair.

≣ PRIORITIZE COLLECTIBLES
The most important collectibles unlock new characters and items.

≣ KEEP MOVING
When you get to a stage's end, keep moving to avoid the projectiles your enemy throws.

≣ GRAB BATARANGS
When you're playing as Batman, collect Batarangs to be rewarded with bonus studs at the end of the stage.

SONIC DASH 2: SONIC BOOM

THE RING LEADER

Sonic has always been about speed, so putting the lightning-fast hedgehog in an endless runner for his jump to the mobile version makes perfect sense. Switch between lanes in order to dodge spikes, leap over obstacles, and spin attack the robotic enemies in your path as you run along in search of new high scores. Once you unlock more characters, such as Knuckles and Amy, you can switch to those characters to add their special abilities to Sonic's Dash Ring Magnet. Once they are a part of your team, you can then focus on moving your way up the leaderboards and beating your friends' scores.

Grinding rails will help to keep your speed up, and is also really important when it comes to collecting extra rings and finding dash boosts in order to make the game go even faster.

It's up to you whether you decide to go through your enemies or dodge them, but you need to choose fast when you're running at high speed.

› ALSO CHECK OUT

Canabalt

This fantastic 2-D title kick-started the endless runner genre on mobile devices. It has a real "just one more try" feel, so you won't be able to stop hitting the restart button when you fall.

Temple Run 2

The smash hit *Temple Run* has set the template for many 3-D endless runners. It's clearly a huge influence on *Sonic Dash 2*, which shares many of the same mechanics, but in this case you're running from scary monsters.

TIPS & TRICKS

KEEP SWAPPING
You will get offered the chance to swap runners during your run. Take that chance to help you boost your score.

USE YOUR DASH
If your dash is charged and you spot a hard section coming up, activate your dash to slam right through the obstacles!

CAUTION IS YOUR FRIEND
Don't worry about collecting every ring; focus on keeping your run going.

0/10

The cards you play will appear on the board as you unleash them to try and defeat your enemy.

JumpyWizard

7 4:19 PM

≡ HEARTHSTONE: HEROES OF WARCRAFT

PLAY YOUR CARDS RIGHT

For strategy fans, things don't get much better than *Hearthstone: Heroes of Warcraft.* The tactics start when you pick a class. The Mage, for example, is focused on offense, while the Priest is all about maintaining control of the board. There's another layer of strategy when it comes to building your deck. The fact that *Hearthstone* is a virtual card game means that it works beautifully with touch controls on mobile, too!

> ## ALSO CHECK OUT

Pokémon TCG Online

Swap the wizards and monsters of *Hearthstone* for *Pokémon* in this awesome virtual card game where you can trade with and battle against other real players.

Magic 2015

Magic: The Gathering is an incredibly popular card game in real life, but it's also got a mobile video game version that *Hearthstone* fans will enjoy.

≡ BALANCE YOUR DECK
You'll want to have mix of low and mid-tier cards, along with ones with high mana.

≡ HAVE A PLAN
Pick plenty of healing and taunt minions if control is your favored approach.

≡ KNOW YOUR STRENGTHS
You win some, you lose some. Pay attention to what cards work well for you and adjust your deck accordingly.

☰ STACK

REACH FOR THE STARS

It's the beautiful simplicity and quiet satisfaction of building an ever-growing tower that makes *Stack* such a hit. It's the perfect mobile game to play in short bursts when you've got a few minutes to spare. Blocks slide across the screen, and you have to tap to stack them. If you don't get the block perfectly centered, the excess hanging over the edge will be shaved off, making the game harder with every mistake. Chain a few perfect stacks together, though, and the block will grow again, allowing you to recover any ground you've lost and keep on track for a new high score.

STATS

29
unlockable styles to stack

Stack has a maximum score of
10,000

OVER 12 MILLION
players on Game Center

Stack has a clear, minimalist style that suits the simplicity of its quickfire gameplay.

> ## ALSO CHECK OUT

Crossy Road

If chasing high scores in quick-fire mobile games is your thing, we'd recommend this endless arcade-style hopper, where you have to guide an animal avatar safely through hazards.

THEATRHYTHM FINAL FANTASY

Stack has a bit of a rhythm action element to it. If that whets your appetite for more, *THEATRHYTHM FINAL FANTASY* is another fantastic example of the genre.

☰ GET IN THE RHYTHM
There is a rhythm to the speed that the blocks flow at in *Stack*, judge that as a guide to when to tap the screen.

☰ DON'T GIVE UP
There's no need to reset when things go wrong—you can recover by comboing blocks and growing their size again.

☰ STAY FOCUSED
The front corner is the best position to focus on when you are trying to match blocks.

BEST SELF-IMPROVEMENT GAMES

BETTER YOURSELF WITH THESE GAMES!

Who says playing games isn't good for you? There are plenty of mobile games out there that can help you to develop your life skills. Whether you are looking to keep your brain and body active, or want to speak a new language, there are some awesome game apps that help you to learn everything you need to know, and have fun doing it. If you want something different from your mobile gaming experience, these self-improvement games are worth checking out.

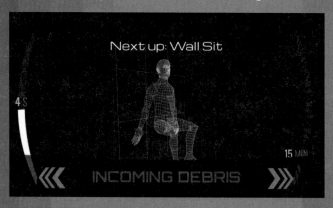

7 MINUTE SUPERHERO WORKOUT

Fight off alien attackers, save the world, and get fit while doing it. *7 Minute Superhero Workout* gives you different exercises to perform, each one helping you to keep a set of invading aliens at bay. If you don't complete your tasks, then your foes will blow up the planet! This motion-tracking workout game helps maintain motivation.

SUSHI MONSTER

To feed Sushi Monster, you need to play through a series of tough games that aim to improve your mathematical skills. You will earn points with each correct answer, but against the clock the game is a lot harder than you might think. Earn enough points and you will face off against Sushi Monster himself.

ELEVATE— BRAIN TRAINING

Elevate–Brain Training is one of the best brain-training apps for smartphone users, and it's free. It keeps your brain sharp, and even tests your reaction skills as you rush to tap the right option. Each section of your brain is challenged in a variety of gaming scenarios, aimed at helping to improve focus, memory, math skills, and vocabulary. Check out the social features, where you can compare your high scores with friends, while also competing on a worldwide leader board.

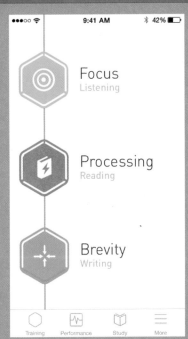

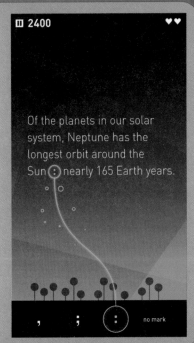

FIT THE FAT 2

Keeping fit is really important, and in this game, the more you exercise, the more weight your virtual friend loses. Think of yourself as his personal trainer—the more active you are, the fitter your friend gets. You must also take care of him, so make sure you feed him properly and keep him entertained during his workouts.

MINDSNACKS

Learning a new language isn't easy, but *MindSnacks* turns it into a game! You can learn everything from Spanish to Japanese. Highly entertaining games for each language help you to test your basic conversation skills. You'll be having such a good time that you'll almost forget you're learning at the same time.

HABITICA

Habitica aims to help you to stay as organized as possible, by turning daily tasks, like doing homework and washing dishes, into a role-playing game. Every time you complete a task, you'll gain experience points, which can be used to power up your fighter, unlock new weapons, and upgrade equipment. Along the way, you'll fight monsters and bosses, but to beat them you'll need to have completed a certain amount of tasks. You can even connect with your friends and help motivate them to complete their tasks before taking to the battlefield and fighting foes together.

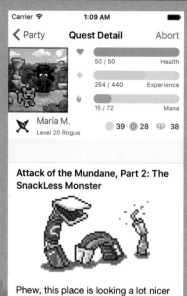

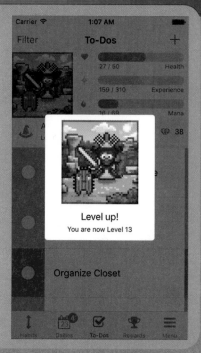

ZOMBIES, RUN!

It's the end of the world, and the only way to fend off the zombie hordes is to run. *Zombies, Run!* tasks you with performing errands in the game by running and exercising in real life. The story is told like an audiobook, and it's so immersive that you'll be running everywhere. It's a great way to get fit while having fun at the same time.

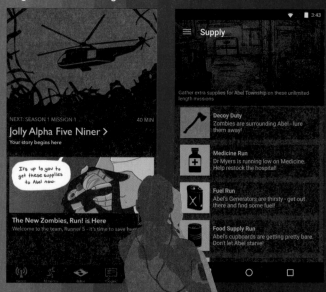

PEAK—BRAIN TRAINING

There are more than 30 amazing games in *Peak*, all of which help to improve your brain in some way. There are word games, to help improve your spelling and memory, but our favorites are number games that make you think fast and react faster—perfect for boosting your gaming skills.

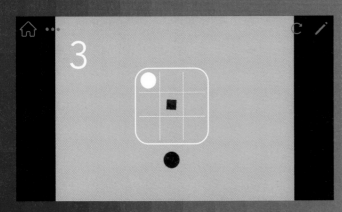

HOPSCOTCH

Coding can be amazingly fun, especially when you can design your own game. *Hopscotch* gives you the tools to learn how to create and code a game, while also playing the games that other people have created. Once done, you can even share your work with other app users.

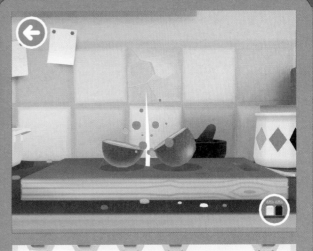

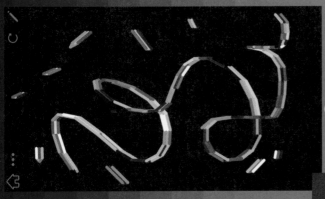

TOCA KITCHEN 2

Follow the recipes to make delicious meals for your virtual family. It's a lot harder than it looks—just one misstep in the kitchen and your virtual family will be left hungry. The game teaches you all the basics of cooking, but without the stress of anyone actually having to switch the stove on!

Mancow

STATS

Your snake keeps growing until it hits a score of
40,000,
after that, the size remains the same but you keep collecting score points

Has a snake snuffed it nearby? Grab the dispersing pellets and you can boost your length by
UP TO 100

At the time of writing, the highest *Slither.io* score on record was a massive
370,232

SLITHER.IO
START SLINGIN' 'EM SNAKES

Despite its deceptively simplistic appearance, *slither.io* **is one of the world's biggest—and best—massively multiplayer games (MMOs).** It's super-slithery fun to play alone or with your buddies, and is available as both a mobile and browser game, so you can slither around whenever you want.

Reminiscent of hit arcade game *Snake*, with simple controls and an even simpler premise, all you need to do is guide your snake around obstacles—and other snakes—to collect the rainbow-colored particles and grow, and grow . . . and grow some more.

Keep on collecting the particles and avoid slamming headfirst into a rival snake, of course, and who knows, maybe you'll eventually grow the biggest *slither.io* snake ever seen.

Careful out there, though—not all snakes are friendly. Avoid being cornered or coiled and you may be able to finish the day off as the world's largest snake (or prevent someone else from taking that honor). *slither.io* is as enjoyable as gaming gets.

> ALSO CHECK OUT

Agar.io
You'll see lots of comparisons to *Agar.io* when you play *slither.io* (and not just the name). Swallow smaller cells, without being swallowed by bigger ones, and keep on growing.

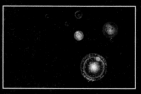

Osmos
 If you like the idea of these games but would rather play alone, try *Osmos*. Like *Agar.io* you can scoff smaller things, but you don't have to worry about being absorbed by other players.

TIPS & TRICKS

≡ DON'T FORGET TO BOOST
Don't forget about your boost, particularly if you're 1000+ in length—it makes for a very fast getaway.

≡ MAP IT OUT
The map is there for a reason—keep to dark areas if you'd prefer to play it safe.

≡ COILING DOWN
If you're feeling brave, trap small snakes or big bunches of particles by coiling gently around them.

The aim of the game is for your snake to be as long as possible without slamming headfirst into other snakes.

TOP 5 SLITHER.IO SKINS

BLOCK SKIN

Playing via Flash? Share the game with your friends and family and you can unlock this super sassy orange and purple skin, complete with unique antenna. With its bold colors and awesome final touches, you'll certainly stand out.

RAINBOW SKIN

Maybe it's the bright, bold combination of colors, or maybe it's just that we're hypnotized when the rainbow snake starts coiling, but there's a special place in our hearts for this fabulously colorful snake.

GLO-WORM/ YELLOW-GRAY SKIN

This yellow-gray skin might not look so special, but we love how magical it looks when you start vacuuming up particles or the remains of your enemies. Flashing until it almost looks translucent, this is one of our favorite unlockables—just share the game with friends to get it.

STARS 'N' STRIPES SKIN

slither.io has colored snake skins to represent lots of different countries, from Britain to Uruguay. This stars-and-stripes skin is designed to represent the U.S. flag—and is one of the most popular choices. Pick a skin from your own country, or just choose a flag you like.

JACKSEPTICEYE SKIN

Representing a famous YouTuber, this skin gets our vote not just because of its awesome color and tone, but also for the fact it sports a super-cool cyclops eye! All the better for keeping an eye out on those competitors, right?

BIG GAMES ON THE SMALL SCREEN

Just because you're playing games on a mobile device doesn't mean you have to leave all your favorite characters and series back at home. Some of gaming's biggest names have made it onto smartphones and tablets, and now you'll find everything from *PAC-MAN* to *Pokémon* on the small screen. Here, we've picked out some of the biggest names to make their way to touchscreen devices, so you can get the thrill of playing console classics on your mobile device, as well as totally new games featuring characters from home consoles.

RAYMAN ADVENTURES

Platforming legend Rayman is back in an all-new adventure for smartphones and tablets. You'll be swinging between trees in the Enchanted Forest and trying to rescue the Incrediballs with the limbless hero. In this mobile game, Rayman gains new powers—by rescuing the helpless balls and hatching eggs—to help him deal with the tougher levels.

ADVENTURES OF MANA

In this remake of a Game Boy classic you must embark on an epic quest to rid the world of the evil Dark Lord of Glaive, fighting monsters, making friends, and finding items along the way. Battles are fast and tactical, and you'll need all your wits about you to make sure you banish your enemies.

VIRTUA TENNIS CHALLENGE

Take to the courts and become the number-one tennis player in the entire world. As you play, you'll develop your character in different areas, allow them to hit the ball harder, move around the court faster, and even perform trick shots. Swiping on the screen makes your character hit different shots—it's a great system.

THE LEGO MOVIE VIDEO GAME

Just like in the movie, Emmet and his friends need to save the LEGO world from the evil Lord Business, who wants to unleash a super weapon called the Kragle. This action-adventure game has platforming and puzzles thrown in for good measure, and features over 90 characters from the movie, just like the console version.

FOOTBALL MANAGER MOBILE 2016

If you want to relive the highs of the soccer season, there's no better way to do it than with *Football Manager*. Take control of your favorite team and guide them to glory using your touchscreen to manage tactics.

STAR WARS: KNIGHTS OF THE OLD REPUBLIC

This title is set thousands of years before *Star Wars Episode IV*, and sees you involved in a massive, sprawling story. Choose a character class and dive into a deep role-playing game ... with lightsabers!

NEVER ALONE: KI EDITION

 Experience the journey of Nuna and Fox, as they search for the source of the eternal blizzard. Players use the touchscreen to control both characters, each with unique skills to help get past certain objects. Expect to explore caves, trek up mountains, and face strange enemies.

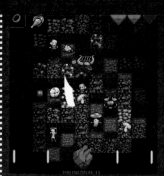

CRYPT OF THE NECRODANCER

This isn't your usual dungeon crawler. Time your moves to the beat of the music and deliver beatdowns to your foes in time with the music. This version is especially cool because it allows you to tap along to any track in your mobile device's music library within the game.

LARA CROFT GO

The famous tomb raider returns in this isometric puzzle adventure. Unlike the main, 3-D games (which are also available for mobile devices), here you must guide Lara through each mazelike level with short swipes and taps. This mobile interpretation of a console classic has won plenty of awards and, if you agree that it deserves them, why not download the free Shard of Life DLC?

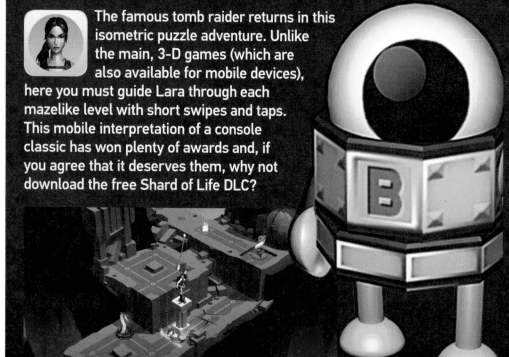

SONIC DASH 2: SONIC BOOM

 Sonic might mainly be known for his side-scrolling adventures, but in this new endless runner you're behind the hero. Sonic (and his friends) sprint through levels collecting rings and using dash attacks to take out enemies.

OCTODAD: DADLIEST CATCH

 He might secretly be an octopus, but that doesn't stop Octodad from being a great father. In this hilarious game, you have to help him live his daily life by controlling his individual limbs using the touchscreen. Just be sure to keep his fishy secret!

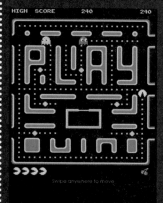

PAC-MAN

 The arcade classic returns with this mobile remake. The original mazes are all here, along with new mazes to try, weekly tournaments, online leaderboards, in-game tips, and achievements to unlock. It's the full PAC-MAN experience, and then some!

FINAL FANTASY III

While there are more than 10 *Final Fantasy* titles currently available for smartphones and tablets, *FFIII* is undoubtedly one of the best. The graphics are cute and colorful, the battle system is incredible, and the option to change jobs as you progress makes this a unique choice.

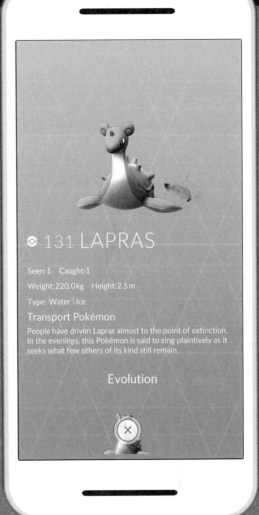

○ 131 LAPRAS

Seen: 1   Caught: 1

Weight: 220.0 kg   Height: 2.5 m

Type: Water | Ice

Transport Pokémon

People have driven Lapras almost to the point of extinction. In the evenings, this Pokémon is said to sing plaintively as it seeks what few others of its kind still remain.

Evolution

WORLD OF GOO

This awesome title first came out on PC and Wii, but proved to be a perfect fit for mobile when it made the jump. Its brilliant physics-based puzzling has been incredibly influential on the mobile game scene. In fact, it even came out before the smash-hit *Angry Birds* bought physics-based gameplay to the masses.

GUITAR HERO LIVE

If you want to rock out with your smartphone or tablet, there's no better way to do it than with *Guitar Hero Live*. You can play it by tapping on the screen, or buy the dedicated guitar controller to complete the game by tapping or strumming rhythms to some incredible tunes.

POKÉMON GO

We've explored many virtual worlds in Pokémon games over the years—from Kanto in *Pokémon Red* and *Blue*, through to the Alola region in *Pokémon Sun* and *Moon*. In making our real world the one that we are exploring, *Pokémon GO* adds a brilliant twist to the familiar Pokémon formula.

SKYLANDERS SUPERCHARGERS

Skylanders' returning villain Kaos attempts to banish the Skylanders from the Skylands by cutting off the portals so that he can rule it himself. But, of course, we can't let that happen! As you platform your way through the world, defeating enemies and bosses, you'll gradually discover that there's even more to Kaos' plot than you first thought—a scary force behind it all.

JUST DANCE NOW

If you already own *Just Dance 2016* on Wii U, Xbox One, or PS4, you can get an app that links to the game and lets you dance while holding your phone. For those without the console game, though, *Just Dance Now* allows you to connect your phone to a smart TV or computer and use your device as a motion-sensing controller as you dance to some massive hits.

SCRIBBLENAUTS UNLIMITED

This is a cool idea. Type a word into *Scribblenauts* and, chances are, the thing you've typed will instantly appear on-screen. Want a corporate werewolf to help you solve the puzzle that you're challenged with? Just type it in, and boom—there it is! The touchscreen controls make zooming in and out and moving the camera around easier than ever before in this mobile version.

ALTO'S ADVENTURE

We absolutely love *Alto's Adventure* and we think you will as well. The game is an endless snowboarding adventure, all controlled simply by tapping on the screen. You must try and correctly time taps to jump at the right time and chain together trick combos. The more combos you perform, the faster you'll go and the better time you'll set on that level. In total, there are 180 levels to complete, each offering a new challenge. It feels a lot like *OlliOlli*, a console hit that sees you skateboarding through 2D levels, and that's no bad thing. In some cases you'll find yourself chasing down runaway llamas, while others will require you to make a leap of a faith off the cliff.

EXPERT COMMENT
ELI CYMET
Alto's Adventure (Producer)

In a way, *Alto's Adventure* is a game that took us two decades to make! Our studio cofounders Ryan Cash and Jordan Rosenberg met when they were four, and grew up together in Richmond Hill, Ontario. As teenagers, they poured countless hours into games like *Tony Hawk Pro Skater*, and spent weekends snowboarding with friends. That inseparability is what led them to found a company together, and in January of 2012, they set about designing *Alto's Adventure*.

Over the next three years, we brought it to life with artist Harry Nesbitt, who took on the programming of the game as well! We've been so floored by the fan response since Alto's release, and think that people really connect with the way the game's art, music, and style capture the serenity and freedom of snowboarding—that moment in nature when everything else falls away. And of course, adorable llamas!

BEST LOCAL MULTIPLAYER GAMES

GAMING IS BETTER WITH FRIENDS

Playing on your own is great, but gaming with friends is a blast! A lot of multiplayer titles require the Internet to connect to friends, but that's not the only way to play. Why not invite some friends over and pass around a single phone or tablet to take turns playing your favorite game? Or you can connect up several mobile devices using Bluetooth and all jump into the same game together.

SPACETEAM

If you've ever watched a sci-fi TV show and wanted to be a crew member on a spaceship, *Spaceteam* is probably the closest you're ever going to come. It's a mobile game built around local multiplayer. You and friends use your mobile devices to take on various jobs on the bridge of a ship hurtling through space. As problems occur, you'll need to work together to solve puzzles before the time runs out. It's incredibly fun and super chaotic, and best played with four other people. Nominating one person as the "Captain" can be useful, so they can issue commands and try to keep order!

TICKET TO RIDE

This pass-and-play digital board game is all about building a railroad empire and taking control of the board. It starts off basic enough, each player collects colored cards, but it's when you start trying to establish train routes across America that it really comes into its own. Win points by completing routes, and beating your friends.

PANDEMIC: THE BOARD GAME

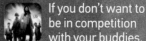

If you don't want to be in competition with your buddies, you should give *Pandemic* a try. Based on a hugely successful board game, it puts you and up to four friends together to try and save the world from a deadly virus. You all share the same screen, doing your best to solve problems as a team and save the world.

WORMS 3

Worms 3 is one of the most awesome multiplayer mobile games the world has ever seen. The game lets you build a custom army of dirt diggers and engage in a little friendly warfare. Not only does it have a great online multiplayer mode, but it also has options to let you and your friends fight it out on the same screen. On your turn, you can move troops and blast away at the enemy with one of the ridiculous weapons. Then, watch your friends take control and throw explosive bananas back. It's chaos!

SLAMJET STADIUM

If you are a fan of air hockey, you will love *Slamjet Stadium*. It's based on the same principle, except now you are playing with another person in real life. The ultimate goal is to flick your car into a goal before one of your friends can do the same—it soon gets frantic and fun, and it definitely takes air hockey to new levels.

HERO ACADEMY

Hero Academy provides light-hearted battles between friends. It's kind of like chess, if chess had animated wizards throwing magic around. You'll need to think tactically if you want to win, but it's quick to learn, and so much fun to play— especially if you have a friend alongside you.

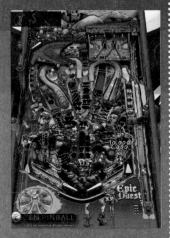

ZEN PINBALL

Pinball has been around for years. In fact, even your grandparents probably played it! Now, you and your friends can enjoy it as well, just sitting on the couch. Set a score, pass the phone over, and watch as your friends try their best to beat it. And with *Star Wars* and *Marvel* tables, the choice is huge.

FRUIT NINJA

One of the most popular mobile games of all time, *Fruit Ninja* also has an awesome split-screen mode, meaning you and another ninja can share a screen as you put your fruit slicing skill to the test. Swipe your finger across the screen to slice the fruit.

BAM FU

Hands (and friendships) will collide in *Bam fu*. Supporting up to four players, *Bam fu* has you flex fingers in preparation for chaotic tapping, with everyone fighting over the same colored pebbles. It gets out of control in the best way; it's the mobile-game version of thumb wars.

DRAWRACE 2

DrawRace 2 is one of the most perfectly designed touchscreen games we've played. You draw your racing line over the track with your finger, and the car speedily follows. It can also be played on the same screen with friends, so you can finally settle the argument: who has the fastest finger?

BEST RHYTHM GAMES

TAP TO THE BEAT

Music games have come into their own on mobile devices. The touchscreen means the games are often simple in spirit, but developers are finding clever ways to combine rhythm and established gaming formats to create an experience you can't find anywhere else. If you're a fan of a solid beat and awesome visuals, these games will have you tapping along in no time at all.

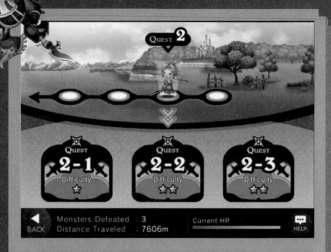

CRYPT OF THE NECRODANCER POCKET EDITION

 If you like a catchy rhythm, then you'll love *Crypt of the NecroDancer*. The game's rhythm-based dungeon crawling takes place in procedurally generated levels that are different every time you play. You never know what upgrades and items you might find.

JUST DANCE NOW

Who'd have thought that the *Just Dance* experience could be so perfectly pared down to work on mobile devices! With great songs including *Happy* by Pharrell Williams, *Let It Go* from Frozen, and classics such as *I Get Around* by The Beach Boys, there is something for everyone to dance to.

THEATRHYTHM FINAL FANTASY

The *Final Fantasy* series has always had some of the finest music in the video-game industry, often mixing sweeping orchestral scores with awesome guitar solos. That's why we love *THEATRHYTHM: FINAL FANTASY*, a game that utilizes the touchscreen to have you tapping and swiping along to some of the series' most famous tunes. Each game mode—from big boss battles to world exploration—has various music tools to learn and master that will keep you entertained for weeks.

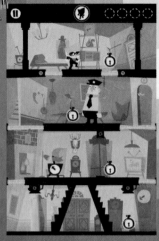

GUITAR HERO LIVE

Whether you're at home or on the go, *Guitar Hero Live* is here to help you rock out. It's essentially a scaled-back version of the full console experience—it lets you play along to songs in front of real crowds and engage in a real-time music channel song select experience. If you own the guitar peripheral already, then you'll be able to sync it up to your device via Bluetooth and rock out without any problems. But if you don't have it, there is also a digital touch-only version available so you can still enjoy the music with just your smartphone in your hand.

GROOVE PLANET

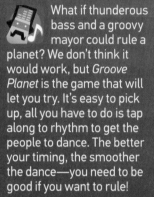

What if thunderous bass and a groovy mayor could rule a planet? We don't think it would work, but *Groove Planet* is the game that will let you try. It's easy to pick up, all you have to do is tap along to rhythm to get the people to dance. The better your timing, the smoother the dance—you need to be good if you want to rule!

BEAT SNEAK BANDIT

This music game seems simple at first, but combined with some great puzzle elements and some great visuals, *Beat Sneak Bandit* works brilliantly. Everything in the game moves rhythmically, and you'll need to tap to the beat to sneak through the tough levels, avoiding enemy guards as you play.

DROPCHORD

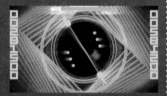

Music and puzzles collide with *Dropchord*. It's a unique score challenge game with mesmerizing visuals, combined expertly with a manic electronic soundtrack. Using your fingers and mastery of motion, *Dropchord* is one of those wonderful experiences you'll only ever find on mobile games.

CYTUS

Cytus is a beautifully strange rhythm game, combining sick beats and a weird art style to create something pretty unique. Notes will move toward a line on the screen and you'll need to use your finger to tap every time a note passes through it. It's tough, but with over 200 songs to choose from, there are plenty of tracks to try.

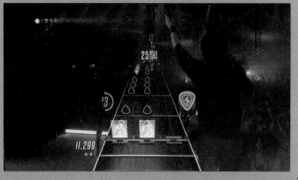

Match up multiple candies to rack up those high scores. The meter in the lower-right corner shows how well you are doing score-wise.

STATS

$318,843
daily revenue estimate

34,888
daily installs

#5
in the top-grossing games

CANDY CRUSH SAGA

SUGARCOATED MATCHING MADNESS

Candy Crush Saga **is so popular that even your parents might be playing it.** So, what's all the fuss about? Well, it's a simple puzzle game in which you have to match up candies of the same color. You only have a limited number of moves to complete each level, so you have to think carefully and plan a few moves ahead to make those screen-shattering mega-matches! It's really easy to get into, but gets really tough after it's got its hook in you!

> ## ALSO CHECK OUT

Dots: A Game About Connecting

This simple puzzle game requires you to link dots of the same color on screen to clear them and hit specific targets. However, with a fixed number of moves it soon gets tricky.

Unroll Me — unblock the slots

This puzzle game challenges you to quickly rearrange the tiles onscreen so that you can form a path for a ball to move into the goal zone. With limited moves, it's harder than it looks!

TIPS & TRICKS

START AT THE BOTTOM
Try to crush candies at the bottom, as dropping candies creates a cascade.

GO FOR COMBOS
Match up multiple candies to create special sweets that clear larger areas of the grid.

CLEAR THE EDGES
When you need to clear jelly, target the edges and corners, as these require the least amount of combinations to clear.

RAYMAN ADVENTURES

OLD TIMER RETURNS TO EPICNESS

When an enchanted forest is in trouble because the ancient eggs needed to sustain the trees have been stolen and scattered across the land, a classic gaming character is called in to save the day. You may not know that Rayman started life on the original PlayStation in 1995, but here he is starring in arguably one of the best platform games available for touchscreen devices. You have to run, jump, and swipe your way through the levels, sniffing out the vast array of secrets and battling unsavory characters, including skeletons, bandits, and mythical creatures. Best of all, it's free to play, so download it today.

☼ STATS

5 WORLDS
to conquer

158
Incredibles to liberate

4 TYPES
of level to play

Getting to the end of the level in one piece is just part of the challenge since each area is packed full of secrets to track down and collect.

› ALSO CHECK OUT

Monument Valley
The goal here is to guide a silent princess through mazelike levels by twisting and contorting the buildings. It's surprisingly absorbing and presents a mind-melting challenge.

Sonic Dash 2: Sonic Boom
Another classic video-game character enjoying something of a touchscreen comeback. The game takes Sonic's traditional platform roots and adds a touch of *Temple Run* to the formula.

TIPS & TRICKS

≡ USE INCREDIBLES WISELY
Incredibles are small creatures that you free and then call on to assist you in levels. One, for example, sniffs out secrets.

≡ INCUBATE THOSE EGGS
Every time you rescue an egg, it will take time to incubate. Pop it into the incubator and leave it—it may hatch into a rare creature.

≡ GRAB THOSE GEMS
Gems are an important currency and are used to buy, among other things, lucky tickets that you can scratch for prizes.

PLANTS VS. ZOMBIES 2

Plants vs. Zombies 2 is without question the most successful zombie game to have ever graced mobile platforms. And it proves once and for all that just because it's a game about the living dead, it doesn't necessarily follow that there's excessive blood and guts. This sequel to the tower defense classic adds a new time-traveling twist, seeing you travel to Ancient Egypt, the Wild West, and more. That means you've got new zombies to deal with including bull-riding zombies, robot zombies, and mummified zombies!

BEST ZOMBIE GAMES

NIGHT OF THE LIVING TAP

The living dead have never been more popular. Despite the fact that zombies can be pretty scary, they've also proven to be a lot of fun in the right scenarios. Whether you're battling against them with mutant plants, farming your own army of biters, or simply smashing every single one of them in sight, zombies have invaded just about every type of game you could imagine.

AGE OF ZOMBIES

Travel back in time and take on prehistoric zombie threats, including, of course, the mighty Zombie T-Rex. *Age Of Zombies* is super silly, there's no doubt about that, but it's also pretty amusing. A frantic twin-stick shooter, it remains simple and fun even as the waves of enemies begin to thicken!

ZOMBIE LIFE

Zombie Life is a bit like *The Sims*, except you aren't trying to integrate yourself into a normal community. No, here you are a traveling zombie, desperately trying to conceal your identity while you look for work, friends, and entertainment. It's quite bizarre, but a very entertaining game.

ZOMBIE FARM 2

Do you want a break from killing zombies? Then why not try farming them instead, in the aptly named *Zombie Farm 2*? This quirky game lets you grow and harvest your own zombies, create new hybrid monsters, and then battle your homegrown army against your friends' creations.

MONSTER DASH

From the team that brought you the brilliant *Jetpack Joyride* comes a zombie-based endless runner with plenty of twists. Whether it's the appearance of Slimer from *Ghostbusters* or the traps that litter the track, you'll need to stay on your toes. You'll speed across rooftops as Barry Steakfries, blasting zombies as you go. Each level offers you a specific challenge, so completing the whole game will take you quite a while!

ZOMBIE SMASHER

Sometimes the simplest of games are the most fun to play, and that's why we're still playing *Zombie Smasher*. Defend your hometown with nothing but your index finger, tapping anything that moves before it can get to your front door. It's silly, but you won't be able to put it down.

PLAGUE INC.

Do you think you have what it takes to infect the entire world? *Plague Inc.* is a blast of high strategy and crazy simulation as you attempt to spread a virus all across the land. Do you have what it takes to end human history with your zombies? It's certainly fun to try.

ZOMBIE HIGHWAY 2

It's fast, it's challenging, and it's got zombies in it—what more could you possibly ask for? *Zombie Highway 2* is an endless runner of sorts, but instead of running you are shooting. Across 67 challenges, you'll need to defend your vehicle against hordes of zombies in this free-to-play thriller.

ZOMBIE CASTAWAYS

Imagine if you were a zombie and you fell in love with a human—would you want to revert back to human form and go live a happy life? Of course you would! That's the twisted scenario *Zombie Castaways* lets you role-play as you farm, explore, and craft your way back into humanity's good books.

STUPID ZOMBIES 3

It's a pretty interesting mashup of ideas, but somehow *Stupid Zombies 3* makes it work. The mobile version of this series has been pretty successful, but the most recent version is without question the best yet, offering up 120 levels of chaos for you to enjoy. It's like a combination of *Angry Birds* and *Worms*, as you try to wipe out the zombies with well-placed shots. *Stupid Zombies 3* is a puzzle game that also includes a whole lot of explosions. Sometimes you can't really ask for any more than that.

There is no dialogue. Instead, the game cleverly uses visual icons to represent each character's thoughts.

STATS

Dropsy's Kickstarter campaign raised
$24,921

57%
of *Dropsy's* Kickstarter backers were from the US

A 16-PAGE
Dropsy coloring book has been released

DROPSY
EVERYONE LOVES HUGS

Dropsy does things a little differently. Unlike most other narrative adventure games, you're free to roam wherever you like, follow the threads you find interesting, and piece together the story as you choose. *Dropsy* further stands out from the crowd thanks to its uniquely quirky world, goofy sense of humor, colorful characters, and distinctive art style. You play as Dropsy, a lovable clown who is on a mission to help those in need, solve some mysteries, and, most importantly, hug everyone he can! Sure, it's a bit odd, but just like Dropsy himself, this game is full of heart.

> ## ALSO CHECK OUT

Grim Fandango
Relive an adventure classic in the form of the remastered version of *Grim Fandango*, where you take on the role of Manny Calavara in a funny and epic journey through the land of the dead.

Machinarium
This is one of the best adventure games released in recent years. Like *Dropsy*, it uses visual icons to communicate, rather than text or speech, and will keep you entertained for hours.

 TIPS & TRICKS

USE YOUR COMPANIONS
Companions like Dropsy's little puppy can reach places that he can't—don't forget to use those abilities!

EXPLORE EVERYTHING
You don't have to solve every puzzle in the game, but the side quests are definitely worth exploring.

TIME FOR CHANGE
Some puzzles can be solved only at certain times of the day. Send Dropsy to bed if you need to change the time.

FIELDRUNNERS 2

NO ONE HERE GETS OUT ALIVE!

This tower defense game requires you to set up various turrets around the game maps to prevent enemy troops storming from one side to the other. You have to contend with ground troops, tanks, choppers, and more, and must strategically place your armaments along the routes they pass through to inflict damage. You can reposition defenses as you see fit and use money earned from defeating enemies to upgrade the turrets. The challenge starts off fairly relaxed, but is soon ramped up when the enemies start to storm in greater numbers.

:::STATS

25
varied battlefields

20
upgradable weapons

3 LEVELS
of difficulty

The enemies soon start to come thick and fast, so you will need to line the escape routes in order to bring them down successfully.

› ALSO CHECK OUT

Plants vs. Zombies
This tower-defense title helped to kick-start the genre's popularity and is still one of the most fun. The franchise has recently expanded to include a shooter on Xbox One and PS4!

Castle Defense
With orcs, goblins, and loads of other monsters attempting to storm your kingdom, you have to repel them using a wide variety of towers. This is a must-have, and it's free to play!

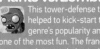

TIPS & TRICKS

≡ REPOSITION YOUR TURRETS
If a turret isn't being maximized in its current position, then you can sell it and reposition, although doing this incurs a point penalty.

≡ PAUSE FOR THOUGHT
Don't be afraid to pause the game at any time to give you some valuable time to rethink your defenses.

≡ REPLAY THE TUTORIAL
When starting out, replay the tutorial level on the Heroic difficulty to earn more stars to buy better turrets early on.

When a new item has been created, you can drag it into position to make use of it. Any unwanted items can be trashed at any time.

:STATS

1,000+
items to create

5
worlds to conquer

50+
levels to beat

> ## ALSO CHECK OUT

Drawn to Life
This blend of sidescrolling platformer and top-down RPG lets you draw your own characters and items to appear in the game.

Terraria
Just like *Scribblenauts*, *Terraria* is a game that relies on your imagination and creativity. It's a more dangerous world to explore, but what you decide to build is up to you.

SCRIBBLENAUTS REMIX

HIGHLY IMAGINATIVE PUZZLE FUN

Scribblenauts is a puzzle game with a difference—you create the items you need to solve the problems put in front of you. Do you need to deal with a monster? You could type in "Shrink Ray", then use it to shrink the monster. Or you could summon a dinosaur to take it on. It's down to your imagination and creativity to find a solution. With 40 levels from the first two *Scribblenauts* games, plus 10 created for mobile devices, there's plenty for you to try.

SECRET LEVELS
Spawn a teleporter to access secret levels or a time machine to visit medieval or prehistoric times.

EASY MONEY
Go to level 10-11 in Action mode and then walk towards the star and finish the level. Do this repeatedly to receive a lot of "Ollars".

EASY KILLS
The Blob is immune to most attacks, so transport him around the level defeating enemies to give yourself a clear path.

MOMOKA: AN INTERPLANETARY ADVENTURE

AN ENGAGING SPACE SHOOTER

With a solar system full of planets to explore, *Momoka* neatly combines platform and shooting action with RPG elements. The 2-D graphics are simple but effective, as you bound around exploring the planets on foot before flying off to new ones. You can skip between planets freely, but the ultimate aim is to discover the reason for the Sun burning out and avert the disaster. Along the way you will encounter fellow space travelers, and no shortage of fearsome enemies to combat. It's a Metroidvania at heart, and the universe you can explore is a really impressive size for a mobile game. Highly recommended.

:STATS

20+
planets to explore

10+
upgrades to collect

8 HOURS
to complete

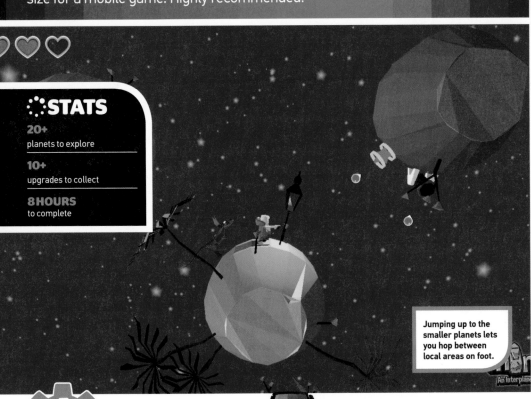

Jumping up to the smaller planets lets you hop between local areas on foot.

TIPS & TRICKS

≡ EXPLORE FULLY
Make sure you search every area and talk to everyone you encounter, since they can provide items and advice.

≡ USE THE GRAVITY SPHERES
You may get confused about where to go in the first area. Look up to see charcoal-gray spheres that you can jump on to progress.

≡ NESTS BREED HEARTS
Destroying small enemy nests will get you a bonus heart. Also, look for canisters to increase your health capacity.

COOLEST CONTROL SYSTEMS

MORE THAN JUST TAP, TAP, TAP

Touchscreens are a very unique type of control method. If you've got a games console or PC, then you're probably used to pressing buttons, twiddling joysticks, or clicking mice. That's not possible with a touchscreen, so developers of games on mobile devices have to be a lot more inventive with their control schemes. A great use of the touchscreen can make a game even better, so we've gathered up the very best games with the smartest use of the technology that we've seen, so you can try them all.

MONUMENT VALLEY

SPIN AROUND AND AROUND

You can interact with practically everything in this game. By the end, you're spinning walkways, twisting ladders, and unveiling hidden paths. Best of all is how this easy-to-control manipulation works together, and how your character interacts with it. The game is about perspective, so if it looks like a bridge is next to a path, your character can step on it. All these interactions aren't just for fiddling with the screen, but for careful positioning so that you can make a route to the exit.

BLOWN AWAY: SECRET OF THE WIND

INTO THIN AIR

 The addition of teleportation shoes—so you can touch anywhere on-screen and appear there— is an interesting new mechanic for a puzzle platformer. It requires you to be precise to succeed, too, so don't think it's easy just because you can teleport.

DOES NOT COMMUTE

A PILE UP

 In this game each vehicle handles differently from every other and you need to guide each car, boat, or bike individually toward its destination. It's not easy, as it's very crowded and you only tap to steer left or right—there's no speed control here!

CUT THE ROPE 2

SLICE AND DICE

 Cut The Rope 2 expands on the beautiful simplicity the first game's puzzle mechanics with a more in-depth story, new characters, and more detailed environments to feast your eyes on. Of course, it's still about cutting the rope and getting the candy into a cute little monster's mouth with a swift swipe of the finger, too!

LEO'S FORTUNE
PUFFER UP

If a game's controls are so natural that you don't think about them when you're playing, you know they have been designed well. *Leo's Fortune* is one such game, in which all you need to do is hold the touchscreen and swipe in the direction you want Leo to travel. From there, the fluffy ball will roll until stopped, with further taps and holds helping to propel the guy into the air where he puffs up and gently floats to the ground. You don't need to do much to play *Leo's Fortune*, and yet it still manages to be a challenge. It proves that you don't need lots of complex mechanics and systems for a game to work well.

SOLIPSKIER
HIGH-SPEED SKIING

All you do here is hold the screen, creating a route for your skier to ride across. Sound easy? Well it's not, because it's up to you to create slopes for speed, jumps to clear gaps and—sometimes—lines to score big in tunnels. And you must do all this simply by sliding your thumb up and down.

STACK
IT'S IN THE TIMING

This game revolves entirely around its control scheme. The whole point is to tap anywhere on the screen to drop the moving block on top of your ever-increasing tower. The skill comes in the timing, but once you master that and the tapping, you'll just want to beat your high score.

TACTILE WARS

DRAWING THE LINE

Patterns might not sound very exciting, but in this game that's how you control an entire army. The game has you designing specific patterns for your army to fight in, and you must ensure they're as good at defending as they are at attacking. As a result, *Tactile Wars* is like a puzzle game, combining smart thinking with clever controls to create a unique strategy game for mobile devices.

THE FIRM

BUY OR SELL?

Left or right, that's as difficult as *The Firm's* control system gets. That doesn't mean it's not an intense game though—you have to sort your big corporation's files, and the pressure is on. Swiping the wrong way feels truly awful, and that says a lot about how great game design can make even two choices in controls feel important.

MONSTERS ATE MY CONDO

HUNGRY, HUNGRY MONSTERS

This is kind of the opposite of *Stack*, because you take slices away instead of building them on top of one another. It's a fun and colorful way of playing, but the controls themselves are so tactile that sliding a piece away with your touchscreen almost feels like you're playing a game of *Jenga*.

SHOWCASE
MONUMENT VALLEY

Monument Valley has taken the world by storm with its incredible, mind-bending 3-D puzzles and beautiful art style. You control Princess Ada as she travels through odd, seemingly impossible geometric worlds to reach the exit. Here, we glimpse behind the scenes to see how a crazy idea for a game developed into such a huge hit.

16-Sept

The developers decided at the start of the project that every screen in the game would be a work of art on its own. They wanted every screenshot to look so good that it could be printed and hung on a wall like a poster.

In the early stages of the creation process, the heroine, Ada, was envisioned playing a musical instrument and carrying items to finish levels.

The team behind *Monument Valley* worked on dozens of levels during development, but only the very best made it into the final game. Their standards were extremely high.

The team were inspired by artists like Oscar Reutersvärd and M. C. Escher, who drew "impossible shapes." The team re-created these shapes in 3-D, and expanded on them to create levels.

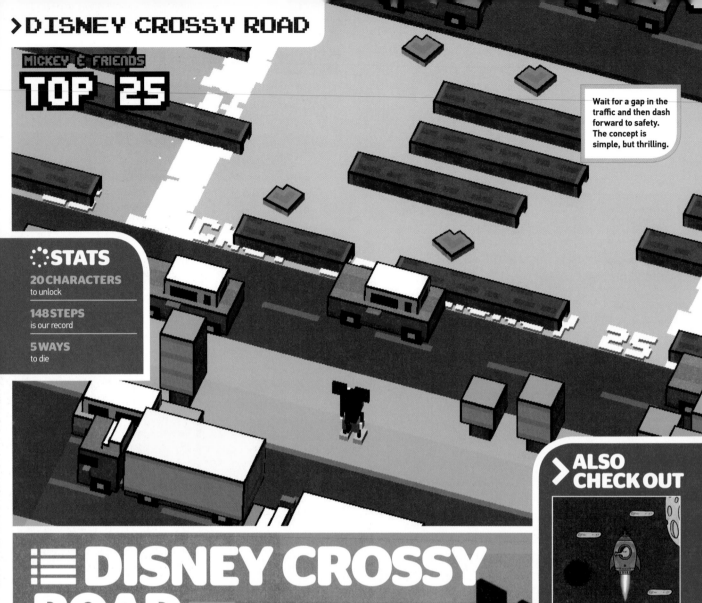

MICKEY & FRIENDS
TOP 25

Wait for a gap in the traffic and then dash forward to safety. The concept is simple, but thrilling.

:∴:STATS

20 CHARACTERS
to unlock

148 STEPS
is our record

5 WAYS
to die

≡ DISNEY CROSSY ROAD

REMEMBER TO LOOK BOTH WAYS

Disney Crossy Road presents a world filled with things to cross, and your aim is to survive for as long as possible. In this game there are roads filled with endless streams of traffic, railway lines and rivers—you simply have to time your progression and aim for the gaps. It sounds easy, but you have precious little time to stop and think—take too long to move on and an eagle will swoop in, forcing you to restart.

> ALSO CHECK OUT

Doodle Jump
Crazy power-ups, such as rockets and spring-powered shoes help you in your quest to reach the highest point possible in this game. It's similar to Crossy Road, but vertical.

Smashy Road: Wanted
Take a ride on the wrong side of the law. Buckle up and see how long you can survive on the road while being relentlessly pursued by police cars, SWAT teams, and even tanks.

≡ TIPS & TRICKS

≡ COLLECT TOKENS
Try and collect any tokens you see lying around, as these can be spent in the vending machine to unlock extra characters to use.

≡ LOG OFF
Don't stay on the floating logs for too long. If they get close to the edge of the screen, then it's game over.

≡ TAP FAST
Tapping and swiping will speed up your movement, so be quick when you only have small gaps to get through.

≡ FTL: FASTER THAN LIGHT

A TRIP THROUGH THE GALAXY

FTL

Get chased across the galaxy in this difficult space strategy game. You have to survive eight procedurally generated sectors on your way to the Galactic Federation. The touchscreen controls are perfect for this strategy simulator. You have to outfit and upgrade your ship and recruit crew to give you the best possible chance of surviving real-time combat encounters with rebel ships. It's a very challenging game as the rebels will try and shoot you down or even board you. Don't be surprised if it takes you quite a few tries to refine your strategy and finally succeed.

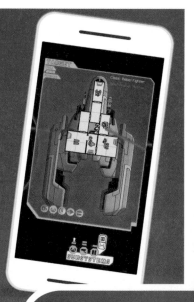

⁝⁝⁝ STATS

SEVEN
alien races to recruit

1 CHANCE:
if you fail you have to start again from the beginning

EIGHT SECTORS
to conquer

If your ship gets set on fire, you can send your crew to put it out, or open doors to suck out oxygen and put the fire out.

> ## ALSO CHECK OUT

Out There: Ω Edition
Take part in another journey across space, during which you can explore planets and meet a range of aliens. Taking risks is a key part of this game, just like in *FTL*.

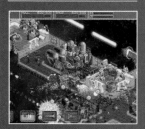

Star Command
This games shares loads of similarities with *FTL*. You build your own ship, recruit a crew, explore the universe, and get in lots of trouble battling aliens!

TIPS & TRICKS

≡ **UPGRADE YOUR DOORS**
If you don't have upgraded doors then you will be very vulnerable to invaders and fire. Get it done as soon as you can!

≡ **FOCUS ON ENGINES**
Placing a crew member in the engine room increases evasion, which can be better than focusing on your shields.

≡ **SCAN YOUR FOES**
The icon below an enemy ship tells you what systems they have, and helps you plan what to focus on.

CSR CLASSICS

 CSR Racing may be one of the classics, but this vintage take on the drag-strip formula is a wonderful update. It's a game based around momentum, acceleration, and perfectly timed gear shifts. Jump in some of the most legendary cars ever to grace the road and tear it up in style.

HOVERCRAFT: TAKEDOWN

 If you're a little bored of traditional track racing, you should check out *Hovercraft: Takedown*. This colorful, blocky racer combines speedy action with thrilling combat. *Hovercraft: Takedown* also gives you the opportunity to design your own vehicle. Load it with weapons to suit your style and then hit the grid in force.

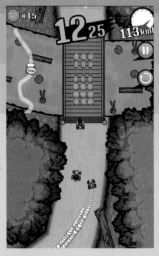

FRZ: FREE RACING ZERO

 FRZ is a homage to a retro game, *Micro Machines*. Both games let you crash around tight tracks, with sharp turns and competitive opponents. This top-down racer is best enjoyed in sharp, focused plays—especially if you want to climb higher in the online leaderboards.

ASPHALT 8: AIRBORNE

 Everything about *Asphalt 8: Airborne* is tailored towards giving you the best handheld racing action. It is one of the longest-established racing franchises, and you can expect blazing speeds, lush graphics, a comprehensive career mode, and an array of customization options to exhance your experience.

BEST RACING GAMES

BURNING RUBBER ON THE SMALL SCREEN

Gamers used to think that racing games were best suited to a gamepad or racing wheel, but that's no longer true. These ten racing games prove that mobile devices and touchscreen controls have plenty to offer the genre. Whether you are looking for a quick taste of thrilling action or something deeper to sink your teeth into, there is something for everyone in the mobile racing category.

NEED FOR SPEED NO LIMITS

Need for Speed may look a little tired and old on console, but this legendary franchise has made an awesome transition to iOS and Android devices. The *Need for Speed* series focuses on letting you burn rubber through tight, beautiful urban environments—and *No Limits* is certainly no slouch in this department. It's fast, fun, and frenetic action that you won't want to put down. Not only will you find an expansive career mode to enjoy, but there's also a wealth of car customization options. This is console-quality racing on the smaller screen, and it shouldn't be missed.

TRAFFIC RIDER

You don't see a lot of these on mobile devices, but first-person racing works perfectly if you've got a phone with a decent-sized screen, or you're playing on a tablet. In *Traffic Rider* you're on a motorbike, zipping between congested roads, taking on daring overtaking maneuvers, and doing your best not to crash.

HORIZON CHASE —WORLD TOUR

This is one of the best-looking racing games we've seen on a mobile device, but not in the traditional sense. It's got an awesome 16-bit graphical style which matches its stripped-back, super fun handling mechanics. The touchscreen controls take time to master, but it's well worth the effort.

REAL RACING 3

Real Racing 3 from EA feels generations ahead of the competition. It sets a standard by which all other racing games playable on a mobile device should be judged, stunning with its beautiful graphics and slick handling. Based around road and high performance sports cars, the realism and speed it offers needs to be seen to be truly believed. It offers plenty of depth—giving you the option to upgrade your favorite vehicles as you move through various competitions.

ANGRY BIRDS GO!

It has been around for a while, but *Angry Birds GO!* continues to get new updates, making it one of the most content-complete racing games available. Familiar characters, tons of racers, and a huge array of social integration come together to ensure that *Angry Birds GO!* is perfect for your pick-up-and-play gaming sessions.

RIPTIDE GP2

If you're after a real challenge, give *Riptide GP2* a try. It's quick and demands close attention, but you'll be rewarded with an incredibly fun water-based racer. Get good, upgrade your jetski to make it more powerful, and take on your friends in epic battles.

BEST JAPANESE GAMES

UNMISSABLE GAMES FROM JAPAN

You can find great mobile games that have been developed all over the world, but there's something really special about many of the games from Japan. They have quirky, unusual stories, cool characters, and all-new game mechanics. In fact, many Japanese games deliver experiences we've never seen before. You need to check these games out, especially if you're looking for something a little different on your smartphone.

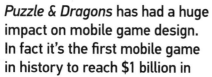

PUZZLE & DRAGONS

Puzzle & Dragons has had a huge impact on mobile game design. In fact it's the first mobile game in history to reach $1 billion in revenue, and that's because this puzzle game is just pure fun. While it seems quite simple on the surface—move and match colored orbs arranged in a grid, like many other games you might have tried—your success increases the attack damage your six dragons do against your enemies. It's hugely replayable and surprisingly deep.

TERRA BATTLE

Produced by the original creator of *Final Fantasy*, *Terra Battle* is a tactical RPG set across a static grid. Using tile-based tactics, *Terra Battle* earns its place in your collection through its super fun puzzle and collectible card game elements. This is an underrated gem that will test both your skills and your patience.

NEKO ATSUME: KITTY COLLECTOR

What a bizarre, but lovely game that fits perfectly in your pocket. *Neko Atsume* has you luring cute cats to your backyard with delicious treats and toys and then doing your best to make them stay. It has all the delights of owning a cat, but without any of the fur balls.

FINAL FANTASY IX

Final Fantasy is one of the biggest franchises in the world and it arrived on mobile devices in style. *VI* and *VII* were great, but it's the ninth installment that will really grab you. The controls work with grace, and you can turn off random encounters if you just want to soak up the incredible world. It's a stunning, deep, JRPG.

DODONPACHI BLISSFUL DEATH

Look past the retro graphics and you'll find one of the most challenging and replayable games available. *DoDonPachi* is a legendary shooter, forcing you to take control of a ship through exhilarating, projectile-filled screens; it's a real skill test.

HEAVENSTRIKE RIVALS

If there's one developer that knows how to create a deep, tactical RPG, it's Square Enix. Quick to learn but deep with strategic possibilities, *Heavenstrike Rivals'* player versus player combat is constantly engaging, hugely enjoyable, and it'll certainly keep you busy for hours.

THE WORLD ENDS WITH YOU: SOLO REMIX

If you ever wanted a window into Japan's unique culture, you just need to play *The World Ends with You*. It's an action RPG that leans heavily on urban fantasy elements. The narrative is fantastic.

GHOST TRICK: PHANTOM DETECTIVE

If you're bored of simple pick-up-and-play games and need for something a little deeper, *Ghost Trick* is for you. It's a quirky story about a ghost seeking answers and trying to save lives.

MONSTER STRIKE

One of the most popular games from Japan, this is another smart puzzler that will keep your fingers as busy as your brain. A basic tile-matching structure combines well with the ability to aim and flick monsters on the field.

ACE ATTORNEY: PHOENIX WRIGHT TRILOGY HD

If you've never owned a Nintendo DS, there's a chance the *Ace Attorney* franchise passed you by. But now the *Phoenix Wright Trilogy* arrives in style. Play as a rookie lawyer defending the innocent in 14 exciting cases, investigating crime scenes and talking to the courtroom.

:::STATS

77 UNLOCKABLE
characters

LEVEL 80
is the level cap

£79.99:
most expensive
microtransaction

☰ STAR WARS: GALAXY OF HEROES

THE FORCE IS STRONG WITH THIS ONE

Galaxy of Heroes might just be the *Star Wars* game we've always dreamed of playing. It's purposefully designed to let you revel in the awesome universe, build mighty teams of your favorite heroes (and villains), and attempt to craft the ultimate strategy to conquer the universe . . . well, the leaderboards at the very least. Using a fun and intuitive turn-based RPG combat system, you'll have to assemble a team, level them up, and then take on some of the galaxy's greatest foes from the perspective of either the Light or Dark side. This is one of those games that's difficult to put down once you pick it up, and before you know it, all of your spare time will have been swallowed into a Sarlacc pit.

TIPS & TRICKS

☰ **DO YOUR DAILIES**
Try to complete every daily goal thrown your way for a quick way to amass important items.

☰ **GET THEM ALL**
Having a deep and varied roster of characters to choose between is helpful.

☰ **BLUE METER WATCH**
The blue meter notifies you when a character is ready to attack. Focus your hits on the enemy closest to recharging!

TOP 5 CHARACTERS

You can play as all your favorite characters from the *Star Wars* universe, including those from the new movies.

PRINCESS LEIA

Leia might be a diplomat in the original movie trilogy, but she is one of the most combat-adept characters in *Galaxy of Heroes*. While Leia can be expensive to level up, she will seriously bolster the offensive capabilities of your squad with her stealth and multi-hit attacks.

OBI-WAN KENOBI (OLD BEN)

One of the all-time greats, Obi-Wan Kenobi has some serious Jedi Mind tricks up his sleeve. He's tricky to level and gear, for sure; but his crippling offensive capabilities make him a must-have addition.

ROYAL GUARD

One of the first Dark Side characters you'll be easily able to get your hands on, the Royal Guard is a must-have addition to any team. Working as a durable tank, you'll be able to easily manage tough fights with the Royal Guard's taunt and stun moves.

REY

The Force Awakens' lead is one of the very best characters you could hope to add to your Light side squad. If you're able to put the time in to level Rey up past level five, and if she's suitably geared up, she will be a near-unstoppable force.

GEONOSIAN SOLDIER

The Geonosian Soldier—from a race that first appeared in the prequel trilogy—is a surprise star of *Galaxy of Heroes*. Get this winged marksman leveled up and you'll struggle to find a character with better agility or survivability. Put the work in and you'll see some fantastic results.

Day 15

It may be tough to survive, but you can build yourself a nice little stronghold if things go well.

STATS

15 PLAYABLE
characters

FOUR
giant boss monsters

Winter lasts
16 IN-GAME DAYS

DON'T STARVE: POCKET EDITION

WINTER IS COMING

Starvation is a very real threat in this hostile world where resources are scarce and monsters are everywhere. That challenge is what makes this survival game fun. *Don't Starve* tells you almost nothing, and we love it for that—it means that you're left to discover what you can craft, farm, build, hunt, and fight. You learn something new on every run, and come back for your next shot at survival with new skills to help you last a few days more.

TIPS & TRICKS

PREPARE FOR WINTER
Start preparing for winter as soon as possible by making warm clothes, crafting a Thermal Stone, and stockpiling food.

DON'T GET SMART
Overconfidence puts you on a road to failure. It only takes one mistake for your game to be over.

FOLLOW THE BEEFALO
It's a good idea to set up base close to Beefalo (not *too* close); their manure is very useful for farming.

JETPACK JOYRIDE

HOW FAR CAN YOU GO?

Evil scientists have developed top-secret jetpacks for evil gain. But it's all right because Barry Steakfries has broken into the lab to steal them—the only problem is that it's a long way back out again. As obstacles such as laser trip wires and missiles come thick and fast, you have to press and hold the screen to use the jetpack to dodge them. You can pick up special vehicles to use for a limited time, and collect coins to spend on enhanced jetpacks and special costumes.

You can also undertake special missions to earn bonus coins, and grab spin tokens to use in a slot machine when you die. The aim is to survive for as long as possible, but that's much easier said than done when you get beyond 5,000 meters!

⚙ STATS

10 JETPACKS
to unlock

18
special gadgets to buy

5,183M
is our record to beat

You can collect bonus vehicles to make it easier to collect coins, and if you get hit, you'll lose only the vehicle, not your life.

If you can manage to collect all the parts of the cool robo suit, then you can simply bat enemy missiles away like they are slightly annoying flies buzzing around your head.

› ALSO CHECK OUT

Color Switch
This game requires you to tap the screen to move your ball up through colored shapes—but the twist is that your ball needs to be the same color as the obstacle to pass through.

Banana Kong
You need to run, jump, bounce, and swing your way through the onrushing terrain by tapping or swiping the touchscreen, and try to cover as much distance and collect as many tasty bananas as possible.

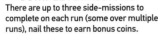

TIPS & TRICKS

≡ COMPLETE MISSIONS
There are up to three side-missions to complete on each run (some over multiple runs), nail these to earn bonus coins.

≡ TIME YOUR SPINS
Wait until the penultimate downward arrow is illuminated on the slot machine before pulling the lever to stand more chance of winning.

≡ SAVE UP
Save up enough coins to purchase the Coin Magnet as this gadget will allow you to collect more coins even faster.

Getting through the levels involves trigger switches, squeezing through gaps, or just bulldozing your way through the scenery. But falling behind means game over.

STATS

40 LEVELS
to complete

27
achievements to earn

80,000+
online players

> **ALSO CHECK OUT**

Leo's Fortune
Like *Badland 2*, this is a physics-based platform game in which you have to survive various traps, solve taxing puzzles, and conquer a variety of lush-looking levels.

Chameleon Run
Requiring laser-sharp vision and ninja-like reflexes, this game asks you to switch color to match the ground while trying not to plummet to a game over through the gaps.

BADLAND 2
BE QUICK OR BE DEAD

With simple two-button controls to hop/roll left or right, the goal of *Badland 2* is to swiftly conquer the hazardous terrain as quickly and effectively as possible. You will encounter obstacles to get around, gaps to squeeze through, and switches to trigger. All of these will help you find passages and routes through seemingly dead-end areas as you attempt to nail each of the taxing single-player levels. There are also online challenges to undertake, such as surviving the longest and rescuing the most clones, as you attempt to storm up the leaderboards. It's great fun!

TIPS & TRICKS

LOOK FOR SOLUTIONS
If you get stuck in a particular part of a level, be on the lookout for switches to open up new routes or any avenues you may have missed.

BE SWIFT
Speed is key. Don't take too long getting through a certain area or you will die.

LOOK CAREFULLY
The action doesn't start unfolding until you make a move, so look closely at your surroundings and make a plan first.

GEOMETRY WARS 3: DIMENSIONS

SUPER-SLICK SHOOTING ACTION

However good you think you are at shoot-'em-ups, nothing can prepare you for the challenge you face here. This game will keep throwing every enemy it can at you from all directions until you lose. Each level consists of a 3-D grid that spawns dangers from all angles, and you have to move all around the shape to dispose of them all and rack up some massive scores. You can also enlist the help of companion drones to attack, ram, snipe, and defend on your behalf, and snare power-ups to increase your firepower. It's a polished, shoot-anything-you-can-aim-at experience that will keep you on your toes.

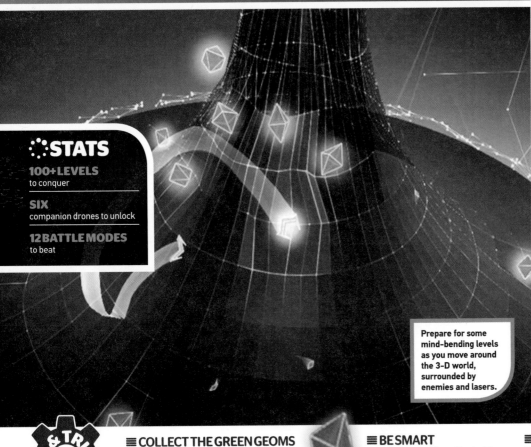

:::STATS

100+ LEVELS
to conquer

SIX
companion drones to unlock

12 BATTLE MODES
to beat

Prepare for some mind-bending levels as you move around the 3-D world, surrounded by enemies and lasers.

> ALSO CHECK OUT

Entwined Challenge
This action reflex game has you controlling two characters independently, the challenge is to guide them through the spiraling levels without your brain breaking in half.

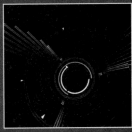

Super Arc Light
Defend your base against endless waves of enemies in this frantic, simple-to-play shooter that takes its inspiration from the original *Geometry Wars* game.

TIPS & TRICKS

≡ COLLECT THE GREEN GEOMS
Make sure you scoop up the green geoms that destroyed enemies leave behind, as these will multiply your score with each subsequent kill.

≡ BE SMART
If you find yourself boxed in, don't be afraid to use your smartbomb to clear the way (and fill the screen with geoms).

≡ USE THE BLACK HOLES
Mainly spawning on Evolved and Deadline levels, black holes will suck all nearby enemies inside, making your life easier.

RETRO GAMES REVISITED

OLD SCHOOL BECOMES NEW SCHOOL

Gaming has been around for many years now; so many years, in fact, that you'll definitely have missed something awesome. "Retro" is a term used to describe old games that can be played only by hunting far and wide for dusty old consoles to play them on. Many retro games have been remade for mobile platforms, which are now powerful enough to run these older titles, and in many cases they've been modernized too. Here are some of the best classic games to try!

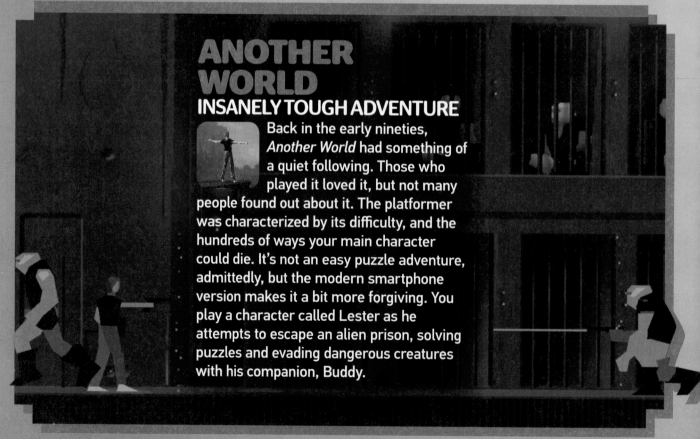

ANOTHER WORLD
INSANELY TOUGH ADVENTURE

Back in the early nineties, *Another World* had something of a quiet following. Those who played it loved it, but not many people found out about it. The platformer was characterized by its difficulty, and the hundreds of ways your main character could die. It's not an easy puzzle adventure, admittedly, but the modern smartphone version makes it a bit more forgiving. You play a character called Lester as he attempts to escape an alien prison, solving puzzles and evading dangerous creatures with his companion, Buddy.

SONIC THE HEDGEHOG
THE BLUE BLUR IS BACK

There are few video-game characters as recognizable as Sonic, and now you can enjoy his best adventures on mobile. *Sonic The Hedgehog* and *Sonic The Hedgehog 2* are both available on touchscreen devices, so you can try out both of these retro classics in one place.

Q*BERT: REBOOTED
YOU'LL SEE BLOCKS FOREVER

You might remember Q*bert from the movie *Wreck-It Ralph*. Well, before that he was a strange creature in this platforming game. This version comes with fancy new graphics, new maps, and items to collect, and it also comes with a classic retro mode that we loved trying out!

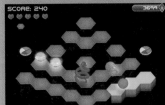

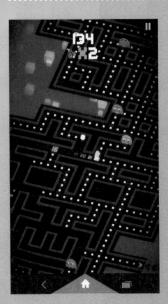
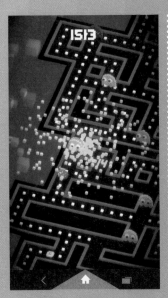

PAC-MAN 256 ENDLESS MAZE
MODERNIZING A CLASSIC

It would be easy to just bring *PAC-MAN* over to smartphones exactly as the game was, but this newer version is so much more mobile friendly. It's an endless runner where you're trying to survive for as long as possible, but with classic *PAC-MAN* gameplay (and a few other new extras, too!)

SKY FORCE RELOADED
SHOOT 'EM ALL

This game used to be huge in the arcades, and if it were brought over to mobile devices exactly as it was, it would be awesome. But the developers have made it even better, improving the controls and updating graphics to make this classic retro game a modern must-play.

CRAZY TAXI CITY RUSH

FASTEST FIRST

This series started in the arcade, and also appeared on the Sega Dreamcast, a console released in 1999. This game re-creates the original's sense of speed and fun, but updates and condenses it for mobile devices. It plays like an endless runner, except you have to swipe to avoid the traffic on the street in front of you. You'll still need to build combos (to earn cash), and get your fares to their destinations on time, but the cool graphics and awesome soundtrack which made the original game so well known have been revitalized.

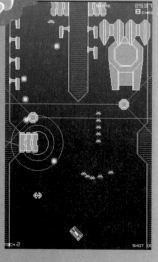

SPACE INVADERS INFINITY GENE

ALIENS ARE COMING

Space Invaders was one of the very first video games, but this revisited version proves that old-school ideas don't have to be old-fashioned. Not only does it look nicer and play much better than its eighties original, but the gameplay itself is far more varied, with different attacks and patterns from the incoming enemies. This is an excellent reimagining of a classic game.

MEGA MAN X
CAN YOU BEAT THEM ALL?

Mega Man was always a tricky platforming game, but it was the boss fights that really stood out as being tough. You'll need to practice and memorize the levels if you want to survive here, but luckily the smartphone controls that have been introduced into the game are great.

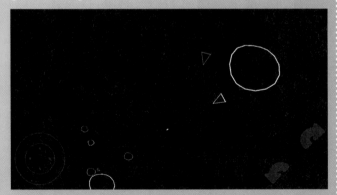

ASTEROIDS
TRULY RETRO GAMING

Before the games industry had really begun, games like *Asteroids* blew people's minds. It might sound crazy when you look at the simple graphics, but just play this classic re-creation of that original game and you'll see why. It's easy to understand, fun to play, and can keep you going for hours as you try to beat your score.

CROSSY ROAD
PLAYING CHICKEN

Crossy Road is based on a famous retro game from the early 1980s—*Frogger*—which tasked you with getting a frog across a busy street and navigating a hazardous river. In this game, you control a chicken trying to cross roads, train tracks, and rivers, and all you need to do is avoid the dangers. Keep playing and you'll unlock lots of different characters to play as.

The aim here is to grow the branches around obstacles and toward the sunlight. But the rate at which the branches grow means this isn't always easy.

> ALSO
CHECK OUT

Tengami
Almost as relaxing as *Prune*, this atmospheric adventure game is set inside a Japanese pop-up book. You have to fold and slide the paper to solve puzzles and discover secrets.

_PRISM
Another great game to zone out with, *_PRISM* presents a sprawling universe contained within geometric shapes. You can push and pull to expand and explore.

≡ PRUNE

NOT A GAME ABOUT DRIED FRUIT

If you're on the lookout for something completely different, then try *Prune*. The aim of the game is to grow a tree and then swipe to cut or "prune" the branches. This alters the direction that the remaining branches grow in and the height that the tree reaches. The purpose of pruning is to help the branches of the tree snake around obstacles and reach sunlight, where it will bloom and scatter its leaves like celebratory confetti. It won't set your pulse racing, but *Prune* is a beautiful, chilled-out game that will make you fall in love with trees.

≡ BLOOMING MARVELOUS
The aim is to get the branches to sunlight to make flowers bloom. Match the amount of blossom with the stars in the sky to complete each level.

≡ TREE GROWING
Pruning some branches will make others grow faster, but don't prune too quickly!

≡ KEEP GROWING
Instead of continuing to the next level each time, continue to grow your tree to unlock special bonuses.

OCTODAD: DADLIEST CATCH

THERE'S SOMETHING FISHY ABOUT DAD

Octodad **isn't your usual adventure.** The main character is an octopus pretending to be a human husband and father. And nobody suspects a thing—even as Octodad struggles to take care of basic daily chores with his eight boneless, flailing limbs. Each of the game's ten levels is made up of simple tasks to complete, but just controlling each of Octodad's limbs independently—even walking in a straight line—is tricky, let alone mowing the lawn or buying groceries. The touchscreen controls take some getting used to, but soon you'll be flailing around like an octo-expert.

:::STATS

12 LEVELS
to complete

39 HIDDEN
ties to find

9 DIFFERENT
formats available

Some levels involve precise movement—not easy when you're controlling an octopus. Try to use very small steps to edge your way through the terrain to your goal.

❭ ALSO CHECK OUT

QWOP
Getting this athlete named QWOP across the finishing line is harder than you think. That's because every limb is controlled individually. You will fall a lot, but that's fine, because it's funny!

Goat Simulator
The goal here is simply to create as much carnage as possible . . . with a goat. *Goat Simulator* is similar to *Octodad* in terms of the wacky theme and the amount of destruction and devastation a simple animal can cause.

TIPS & TRICKS

≡ **OBJECT INTERACTION**
The nearest object you can interact with will glow green. Make slight adjustments to Octodad's arm until this occurs.

≡ **CHANGE THE DIFFICULTY**
Levels will end if you get spotted and exposed too many times. Go to Settings>Difficulty and change it to "Easy" to prevent this.

≡ **FINDING TIES**
Each level contains three hidden ties. You can check which ones you're missing by going to Extras>Ties.

POKÉMON GO

Ever wanted to be the very best like no one ever was? *Pokémon GO* gives you the opportunity to become a real-life pocket monster trainer. Here, catching Pokémon is your real test and training them is your cause. The app uses augmented reality to place Pokémon in the real world, so you can quite literally travel across the land, searching far and wide to complete your Pokédex. Find your favorite Pokémon, train, and nurture them, and become the greatest trainer ever. It doesn't get much better than this.

BEST VIRTUAL PET GAMES

ALL THE FUN WITHOUT ANY OF THE MESS

Looking after pets IRL can be a lot of work. You have to clean, feed, and play with them to make sure they're happy and safe, and that's a big responsibility! If you don't have a real pet, you might want to look after a virtual one on your mobile device. Not only will your new best bud be with you at all times, but you can even look after creatures you can't in real life, like Pokémon!

POCKET PUP

Pocket Pup takes a different route to the usual digital pet games. Instead of simply cleaning and taking care of your puppy, you also complete challenges to teach it new tricks before assembling a 20-page storybook about your new pal to share with your friends.

LITTLE PET SALON

Anyone who's ever been on the Internet knows that everyone loves animals dressed up in stupid costumes! Most pets don't really like dressing up, but these virtual ones sure do. *Little Pet Salon* lets you embarrass the animals and share pics with the world. It's a game full of LOLs . . .

FISH FARM

 Are you looking for a virtual pet game that is all the fun of having a new digital friend but requires virtually zero maintenance? Then you should get yourself one of these gorgeous 3-D aquarium experiences. *Fish Farm* lets you tend to an array of tropical fish. The concept is simple and the experience is relaxing.

MY HORSE

 Horses make special pets, but they are pretty expensive. Thankfully you now no longer need stable space to own one—just enough storage space to download the *My Horse* app. Groom your own horse, enter it into competitions, and open a small window into the world of a real-life horse owner.

Until you found something...

RABBIT EVOLUTION

 Real rabbits might be cute and cuddly, but they're nowhere near as exciting as mutant rabbits! In *Rabbit Evolution* you care for tiny rabbits, use them to win coins, and use science to play with their genetics until you discover all 30 variants.

NEKO ATSUME

 Do you love cats but hate finding fur all over the place? In *Neko Atsume,* fill your garden with beautiful creatures and keep them happy so they stay. It's a simple management game, but it's difficult to put down once you start.

POCKET FROGS —FREE PET FARMING

 A popular mobile virtual pet game, you guide a tadpole into adulthood and command a legion of frogs. Trade with friends and try to fill your "Frogidex" with all 35,000 unique frog species.

MY TALKING TOM

 Adopt an adorable kitten and help it grow into a mischievous cat in *My Talking Tom*. Play mini-games, record videos of your cat's capers, and customize it with over a 1,000 items of fur and clothing. A real cat would never let you dress it up, so seize this opportunity.

TAMAGOTCHI CLASSIC

 *Tamagotchi* is one of *the* all-time classics. Mention virtual pets to anyone over the age of 30 and they will fondly recall the nineties *Tamagotchi* key chains. They let you feed, care, and clean up after your own unique pet. And the experience has been perfectly preserved in *Tamagotchi Classic*. It's as fun as it ever was, making it a simple and endlessly playable game that demonstrates just why this type of game was so popular two decades ago.

You can perform crowd-pleasing tricks off of the stunt ramps to build up your boost meter. You can purchase more death-defying stunts to build your boost faster.

> ALSO CHECK OUT

≣ RIPTIDE GP2

THE WET AND WILD RACER

If you like your racing action full-throttle, high-octane and, um, soaking wet, then *Riptide GP2* is as awesome as it gets. Featuring intense multiplayer face-offs and a full career mode, there is plenty of water-based racing to keep you enthralled. You can also upgrade your rideable hydro-jet vehicle and perform dazzling stunts. Using tilt controls to steer and an auto-acceleration system, you have to concentrate on nailing the perfect racing line through the surf. Performing stunts along the way will build up your boost meter and help you gain an edge over your opponents.

Offroad Legends 2

Conquer bumpy terrain in a variety of monster trucks and 4x4 offroaders. Apply pressure to the accelerator or break pedals at the right times to avoid flipping out.

Slingshot Racing

Employing the novel turning mechanism of latching a grappling hook onto passing posts, this game is a lot of fun. An original alternative to most other racers on the market.

≣ BUY NEW TRICKS
When leveling up, spending your points on high-agility tricks will help you to build up your boost meter much faster.

≣ SAVE UP
There are only a few hydro jets worth purchasing, so save up your money until you can afford the one you really want.

≣ AVOID SOME RAMPS
When going for hot lap speed runs, it is sometimes worth avoiding some of the ramps to maintain a better racing line.

ASPHALT 8: AIRBORNE

THE MOST COMPLETE RACER AROUND

There are thousands of mobile racing games jostling for pole position, but *Asphalt 8* definitely ranks among the best thanks to the depth of cars and tracks available. With over 400 career events and 1,500 challenges to complete, it's not a game you'll master quickly. Plenty of hard work is required to save up enough virtual cash for the hottest motors. *Asphalt 8* handles brilliantly on touchscreen—you can upgrade vehicles to outperform your rivals in the early races and build your way up to the big leagues. There is also online multiplayer with up to 12 real opponents.

2/6 POS.   198 mph   1/1 LAP   00:55:206

METERS DRIFTED
441.12 m

STATS

200+ MILLION
downloads

130+ CARS
to drive

40+ TESTING
tracks

> The tracks take in some lovely scenery—not that you'll have time to take your eyes off the road to appreciate it!

> ALSO CHECK OUT

CSR Racing 2

Delivering super-slick drag racing to your mobile device, *CSR Racing 2* lets you race against live players across the world and build your own supercars to tame the tracks.

Perfect Shift

More drag racing, but this time on testing tracks set around urban environments. It looks fantastic and features fully customizable cars to help you leave your rivals in the dust.

TIPS & TRICKS

≡ SWITCH CONTROLS
The game uses a tilt-to-steer control system by default, but you can switch this to on-screen virtual controls if you prefer.

≡ MASTER THE DRIFT
A tap of the brake button going into bends will start your car drifting. Maintain a drift to earn nitro to boost on the straights.

≡ EXPLORE THE MAPS
The tracks in *Asphalt 8* contain lots of alternate routes and shortcuts. Make sure you keep your eyes open!

21,080 pt

Goal: 50,000 points
3%

Store (tap to buy)
3010

place some grass
1,215 turns left

STATS

150 FREE
turns a day

27 BEARS
needed for a treasure chest

500 COINS
per treasure chest created

Even the enemies have a purpose. Trap the bears and combine three of their tombstones to create a church.

≣ TRIPLE TOWN

SUCCESSFULLY MASHING UP PUZZLES AND BUILDING

This is a strange one—a puzzle game in which you combine elements and items to build a sprawling city. It's kind of like *Candy Crush* crossed with *SimCity*! Bizarrely, it actually works. By grouping together small items, such as patches of grass, you build bigger items that can then be grouped together, and so on until you create buildings and people start to inhabit your city. It's not all straightforward though, as creatures spawn to hamper your progress and restrict your moves, but even these can be turned into structures if you have the skills.

TIPS & TRICKS

≣ OPTIMUM PLACEMENT
Try to build large structures, such as mansions, at the edges of the city, and leave the center of the grid free for expansion.

≣ BEAT THE BEARS
Trap the bears by blocking off their exits. Once they're trapped, a tombstone is formed.

≣ USE THE STORE
Make sure you store essential items, such as diamonds, for later use. Use the small dish in the top-left corner.

THE SIMPSONS: TAPPED OUT

BUILD YOUR OWN SPRINGFIELD

The setup for this cool town-building mobile game is that Homer has gotten distracted while working at the nuclear power plant and managed to wipe out all of Springfield (doh!), leaving you to rebuild it. Every building and shop that you build grants you XP and money. The XP will level you up and unlock more buildings to add to your town, and money provides the means to construct them. You can also complete tasks to earn donuts, which can be used to speed up your builds. Created by the writers of *The Simpsons*, *Tapped Out* is brimming with humor. All of the familiar characters and locations are on hand to help make your Springfield feel as authentic as possible.

⚙ STATS

125 BUILDINGS
to construct

190
characters

9,346
daily installs

By investing enough time into this game, you can create your own living, breathing, fully functioning Springfield featuring characters and buildings from the TV show.

Made by the writers of the TV show, the game is full of the trademark *Simpsons* humor we have come to love over the years . . .

＞ALSO CHECK OUT

Smurfs' Village
Another town-building exercise, this time you're constructing mushroom huts and other structures for the little blue critters and playing fun mini-games to boost your resources.

Farm Story
The challenge in *Farm Story* is to construct your own self-sustaining farm. Grow produce, rear livestock, and try to earn as much money as possible from your efforts to see your farm grow into something special.

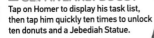

☰ GET AN EARLY BOOST
Tap on Homer to display his task list, then tap him quickly ten times to unlock ten donuts and a Jebediah Statue.

☰ CHOOSE YOUR TASKS CAREFULLY
If you are intending to leave the game for a while, have your characters undertake the more time-consuming, higher-gain missions, to maximize your time away.

☰ LEVEL UP QUICKLY
Make sure you lay plenty of free-to-build items, such as trees and highways, to earn XP to level up more quickly.

BIZARRE SPORTS GAMES

SPORTS JUST GOT KIND OF ODD...

Games like *FIFA* and *Madden NFL* are great fun. But if you want to enjoy something a little different, why not try one of these weird and wonderful games? Whether they've invented their own strange sports, or just added a unique twist to a favorite, these unusual, bizarre, and downright weird games are sure to grab your attention. We've found some of the strangest games that will test your sporting abilities.

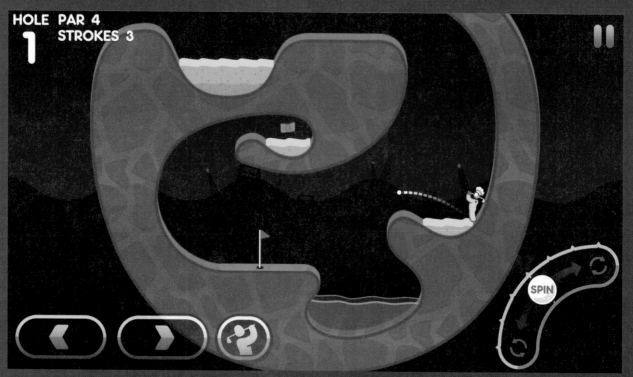

SUPERSTICKMAN GOLF 3
GLUE AND GOLF?

This series of games has been on smartphones for a while now, and the most recent one is the best. It's very simple, you carefully select an angle and then pick the power of the shot. It still plays a lot like traditional golf; the only difference is that ... well, it's sticky. This means your shots land and stay exactly where they are. After the first few holes, you will find more and more challenges to overcome, and you will have to make use of the sticky walls and platforms if you're to finish the level under the shot limit.

SUPER PARTY SPORTS: FOOTBALL

SOCCER NEVER HURT SO MUCH

So, you know *Angry Birds*? Now imagine if that game were played with a soccer ball that is kicked so hard it can knock a player's head from their body! That's the point of this game—you pass between your team, and blast apart the opposition, before scoring a winning goal.

NBA JAM BY EA SPORTS

YOU'RE ON FIRE!

This was a classic on Sega's Mega Drive console, but EA Sports has re-created it with modern graphics for mobile devices. It's an exaggerated version of basketball, with super-big heads, speedy gameplay, and balls that catch on fire when you're doing well.

GOLFINITY

THE SPORT THAT GOES ON FOREVER

Infinity is a pretty mind-blowing concept, and that's what makes *GOLFINITY* stand out as such an unusual video game. Not only is it a great mobile golf game, but with all the crazy loops, bumps, and drops you need to overcome, it's also one of the most interesting. The endless number of randomly generated levels is just a cool bonus.

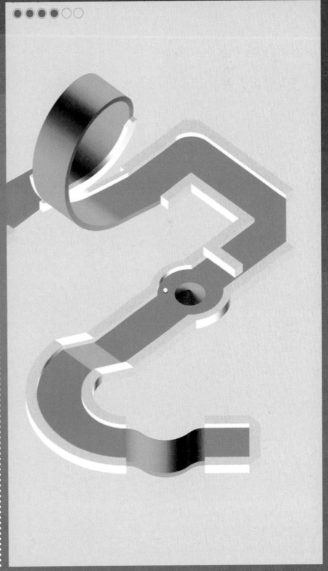

FLAPPY GOLF
BALLS WITH WINGS

There are plenty of *Flappy* games, but they all mostly involve guiding a bird through an endless side-scrolling level. *Flappy Golf* instead takes the core idea of golf—trying to get the ball into a hole marked with a jaunty flag—and adds wings to it, giving you the chance to alter the ball's path by flying through the level. It seems like cheating, sure, but it does require some technique, plus it's super fun.

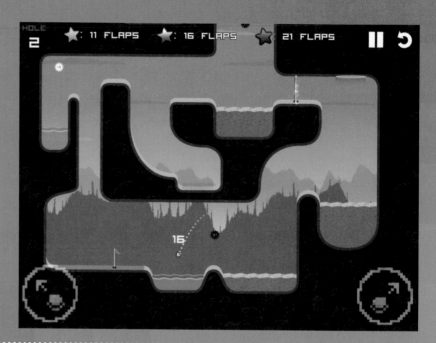

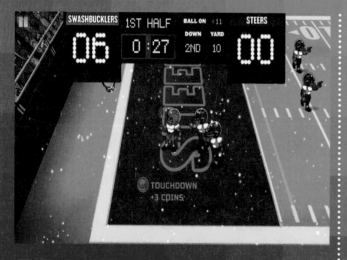

FOOTBALL HEROES PRO 2016

TOUCHDOWNS GALORE!

Football has never been so tough. As you play each game you can use your players' special abilities. These let you charge through opponents, knock them to the ground, break through the defense, or set a ball on fire and launch it across the pitch. It's football, but not as you know it!

BOUNCY BASKETBALL
BOUNCIER THAN NORMAL, ANYWAY

You're probably wondering what's so weird about this one? Well, the crazy physics in this game mean that not only do the players move hilariously, but the points you score will often be totally random. All you do is press one button, but it's still funny to watch your teammates flail around trying to grab the ball. If you do score a three-pointer, you'll cheer and laugh at the same time.

PKTBALL—ENDLESS SMASH SPORT
TENNIS, BUT SO MUCH QUICKER

This game might look cute and colorful, but don't let that fool you—this is also an incredibly cool app. It's a simple idea: just hit the ball back and forth, and as it gets faster and faster, try to angle it just right to hit it past the opposing player. It's quick, it's exciting, and with a variety of unlockables and power-ups, there's always something new to see.

ONLINE HEAD BALL
TAKING "HEADERS" A BIT TOO LITERALLY

Two heads playing soccer? Yeah, this one is really weird. Timing your jumps and kicks is vital in this game, which has online and single-player modes.

POCKET LEAGUE STORY 2
TINY BALLS, HUGE GOALS

The company that made this game—Kairosoft—makes a lot of similar games, and they're almost all brilliant. This one has you managing a team of soccer players as you train them to give them superhuman strength and agility. You'll need to build up a training ground and stadium, hire and fire players, and win as many games as you can. Certain players can have abilities, though, and they'll pull off some amazing, unstoppable shots while they are in their super-powered mode.

SHOWCASE
RAYMAN ADVENTURES

Rayman's home console adventures have been going for decades, and in recent years a beautiful new art style has reinvigorated the hero's quests. Now, we finally have a full *Rayman* game, with this beautiful new art style, available on smartphones and tablets. Here's a closer look at the game's stunning artwork.

Rayman has lots of friends to lend him a hand, including the creatures, who can help him by finding secrets, attracting collectibles, or even attacking enemies.

Rayman originally appeared in 1995, and has changed quite a bit since his debut. In *Adventures,* he can float by spinning his hair, and punch and kick with his huge hands and feet.

If you're thinking that the game looks a lot like a painting, it's because the design team worked hard on a new graphics engine that gives a hand-drawn style.

The puzzles in the game will have you scratching your head. This mobile version will be very familiar to anyone who has played *Rayman Legends* on Xbox One or PlayStation 4.

Crashlands features skill-based combat, but you need to ensure you have the right weapons to take on the game's various enemies.

☰ CRASHLANDS

MAKE YOUR WORLD A BETTER PLACE

It's a hard life being a space trucker, especially when you break down on a remote planet, lose all of your cargo, and get caught up in a sinister plot for world domination. Stuck on a hostile world, you have to harvest as many resources as you can from the terrain. This is used to create equipment to tackle alien adversaries and ultimately blast off of the rock. With RPG elements, skill-based combat, and the resource management of *Minecraft*, there is much to enjoy here as you strive to (literally) build a better future for the planet.

> ## ALSO CHECK OUT

Wayward Souls
This dungeon-plundering game lets you control one of six characters as you battle your way through randomly generated mazelike levels in search of treasure.

Tiny Guardians
Like a tower defense game without the towers, *Tiny Guardians* lets you assemble a crack team of warriors to help you conquer an endless onslaught of tough enemies.

☰ HARVEST EVERYTHING
Hack at everything you find to harvest resources. If you don't have a strong tool yet then be sure to come back when you do.

☰ OBTAINING SCHEMATICS
When you hack at a plant or mineral, or kill a creature, schematics that allow you to craft new items may appear in crates.

☰ RECYCLE YOUR GEAR
You can salvage unwanted equipment by tapping on the recycle icon on the "Flux" screen and then selecting an item.

MARVEL FUTURE FIGHT

LET LOOSE WITH MARVEL'S DREAM TEAM

Bringing together Marvel's best superheroes in one epic scrolling fighting game, *Future Fight* packs one serious punch. You can unlock and team up old favorites such as Captain America and Iron Man with more obscure heroes like Mockingbird and Moon Knight. The graphics are sharp on your mobile device and you can perform some screen-shaking combo moves with the touchscreen to dominate your enemies. The aim is to undertake missions and assemble a dream team of heroes to power through the levels. This is a must for any superhero fan.

⠿ STATS

60 HEROES
to recruit

5 TEAMS
to set up

100+ MISSIONS
to complete

The odds are stacked against you, but by mastering your combat moves and utilizing combos you'll be able to beat your enemies.

› ALSO CHECK OUT

Tap rapidly to boost Damage!

Real Steel Boxing Champions

The ultimate robot-fighting game, you can upgrade and customize your own mech, battle your way up through the ranks, and take on mighty bosses in your quest for steely glory.

DRAGON BALL Z DOKKAN BATTLE

This game takes the insane combat from a popular TV series and applies it to a board-based action game. Assemble your team of warriors and engage in epic, screen-shattering battles.

TIPS & TRICKS

☰ GET THE RIGHT MIX
Adding heroes to your team will provide a team bonus—but some character combos give a bigger boost than others.

☰ FIND THE BIOMETRICS
You can find where your hero's biometric is located by going to Home> Inventory> Biometrics and tapping on the hero profile.

☰ GET SOME REST
When you recruit a new hero, give your existing ones a rest. This helps them recover and achieve "Best Condition" status.

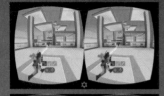

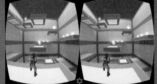

HARDCORE (VR GAME)

 Though you'll need a controller to play *Hardcore*, it's a worthwhile investment. Here you'll have a game that plays just like any typical console game, except with the added perspective of viewing the world in VR. It gives so much more freedom when fighting against enemies, and makes you even more involved in the game.

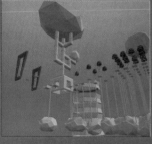

BAMF VR

 There is no better example of how VR can change the way we play games than BAMF. We've seen 3-D puzzle games before, but with the addition of VR, a whole new kind of puzzle is opened up. All you have to do is look at where you want to go and tap to teleport there—it's really intuitive. You really should check this out.

BEST VR GAMES

A NEW WAY OF GAMING

Virtual reality has taken the world by storm by creating digital worlds and using headsets to make them feel real. Now—with inexpensive devices like Google Cardboard or Samsung Gear VR—you can literally see into the games you're playing, and control them with your head. It gives you a whole new perspective to play with, and because of that you'll always have access to truly innovative games. Here's our selection of the very best VR titles.

END SPACE VR FOR CARDBOARD

 Not only does it have intense combat, great graphics, and cool controls, but *End Space VR* has awesome VR features, too. Sitting inside the cockpit of a spaceship really works in virtual reality, and as you peer around at the environment looking around for enemy ships, you'll soon begin to feel like you're actually inside that spaceship. And that's what VR is really about, helping to immerse you so much into the game itself that you actually feel as if you're there. This is perhaps the best example of that on mobile devices yet.

CAAAAARDBOARD!

This game was originally released for PC, but now it can be played with VR and it makes so much more sense. Here you're plummeting down an endless tower, using your head to tilt this way and that to avoid the obstacles in your way. The 3-D movement really helps make this VR game stand out, because it makes you really feel like you're falling down a bottomless pit, which sounds scary—but honestly it's a lot more fun than that. This is a great example of how VR can make an existing game even better.

VOXEL FLY VR

Playing in traffic is a definite no-no in real life, but it's safe to do in a VR game. It's tense, but the unique visual style, the controlled pace of the head tracking, and the comical way the cars pile up when they hit one another makes it a whole lot of fun, too.

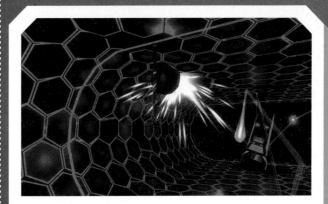

PROTON PULSE GOOGLE CARDBOARD

Pong was one of the first ever video games, and really highlighted what could be done with new computer technology.

Now *Pong* is back to revolutionize gaming, but this time with VR instead. *Proton Pulse Google Cardboard* is essentially still *Pong*, but instead of using a little stick to control the paddle, you use your head in a 3-D environment! Brilliant.

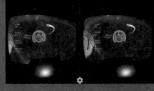

WAA! VR

This is such a simple idea for a VR game, but when you think about it, it's a no-brainer! Asteroids are approaching your position, so you have to tilt your head to find them, lock on by staring at them, and then destroy as many as you can before you're overwhelmed. It doesn't take a lot to figure out, but you'll be trying to beat your score for hours.

RADIAL-G: INFINITY

Endless runners—games like *Temple Run*, that is—aren't too common on VR just yet, but *Radial-G: Infinity* is a great showcase of why they should be.

The fast-paced action of this game makes it very intense to play as you watch the tracks loop in and out of view. It helps that it's a pretty good game by itself, too!

TOP 8 AUGMENTED REALITY GAMES

SEE THE WORLD DIFFERENTLY

When smartphones first came out, people didn't really know the true extent of what they could do. It took a few years to discover their potential, and as the technology became better and better, soon people realized they could use the phone's camera to turn our world—the real-life things in front of us—into games. Augmented reality—or AR as it is known—now takes a variety of different forms, but some of the best uses of it can be found on these pages. From searching for monsters to shooting hoops, they blend the real world with the game world.

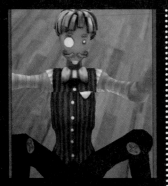

PAPARAZZI-AUGMENTED REALITY

SNAP THOSE CELEBRITIES

Hover some money and a hidden celebrity will appear. From there you must get photos of them by positioning the camera properly. But be warned—do it too much and they may attack you!

PARALLEL KINGDOM MMO

TAKE OVER THE WORLD

This game uses a map of the area around your phone to display an imaginary version of it. There are quests to take on, castles to explore, and monsters to slay, allowing you to level up and build an army. You and your friends can also take over areas of this map.

WARP RUNNER
PLATFORMING, WITH A DIFFERENCE

This is perhaps one of the more innovative AR games out there, because it does something a little bit different. Most AR games are stationary experiences, but not this one. Your character moves around, with the levels that you need to overcome sprouting out of the very world you see right in front of you.

The graphics are especially good, but it's how the AR is used that really impresses, combining a truly great platform game with a very innovative way of playing it. This is one of our favorites.

TOYOTA 86 AR

TURN YOUR DRIVEWAY INTO A RACEWAY

 You will need a pretty large area of space for this game to work, but the local park, your school yard, a wide driveway, or a a spacious patio area would all work just fine. Once set up, you will be handed the controls of a super-fast race car with your mobile device, allowing you to race it around like a digital remote-control car. It's a lot of fun!

AR BASKETBALL

DUNK BALLS INTO YOUR DRINKS

AR Basketball uses your mobile device's camera to turn the real world into a basketball hoop. You need to download and print out a specific piece of paper first, but with it you can position your mobile device itself to get the perfect shots. The hoop moves nearer or farther away as you do yourself. Get slam dunking!

TOY CAR RC

CREATE YOUR VERY OWN RACETRACK

No one really likes putting stuff away, do they? Well, *Toy Car RC* solves that problem, by allowing you to create a digital racetrack out of whichever room you happen to be in. You set down objects, decide on where the corners will be, and then race your toy car. Unfortunately, you'll still have to tidy up the room at the end of the race, but at least you've had fun doing it.

TEMPLE TREASURE HUNT GAME

A REAL EXPLORATION GAME

Perhaps the perfect use of AR, it turns the real world into a treasure hunt. There's some setup involved, but it's worth it, especially when you play with friends. You can hide the pieces of paper that turn the mobile device into a treasure tracker.

POKÉMON GO

GOTTA CATCH 'EM ALL

This is, by far, the most popular AR game ever released. Now instead of playing *Pokémon* on a handheld console, you can play it in real life instead. With this app you're shown nearby creatures to capture, and you need to physically walk to the spot on the map to attempt to capture them. Different areas are home to different Pokémon, so if you want to capture every single one of them, you'll have to head out into the world for real to find them. It's not only a game, but a chance to explore your local area, and a chance to stay fit, too.

As always, you have to carefully aim your bird before pulling back and releasing them to cause as much destruction as possible.

STATS

90 LEVELS
to beat

4
different birds

13TH
Angry Birds game

PIGGY PINBALL ANYONE?

Tying in to the *Angry Birds* movie, this game continues the age-old theme of launching our feathered friends at structures to take down pigs. This time though, the action has shifted to a pinball-style perspective. With pigs positioned around the levels, you have to aim your bird, pull back, and launch, before watching it bound around the screen destroying anything it touches. It's more wonderfully chaotic fun from one of mobile gaming's best-known series.

≡ LINE UP THE PERFECT ROUTE
Pull back and hold before releasing to scan your surroundings and line up the route for maximum damage.

≡ BREAK LOTS OF STUFF
If all else fails, aim your bird into a packed corner and see how much havoc you can wreak—it all helps boost your score.

≡ REVIVE YOUR BIRDS
Save your gems for reviving your birds when you run out of lives. Be careful though; the number of gems required will increase each time.

> ALSO CHECK OUT

Ghostbusters Pinball
 Join up with the original ghost-busting movie crew with this excellent spook-themed flipper-fest that is hard to walk away from.

Zen Pinball
 For more conventional pinball action, look no farther than this awesome sim. It features some engrossing tables with really cool themes for you to try to score big on.

THREES!

WHO KNEW THAT MATH COULD BE SO FUN?

3

Threes! is an enjoyable puzzle game based around math—but before you run away screaming, you should know that it's simple to play and very satisfying. Faced with a grid on which the numbers "1" and "2" appear, you have to swipe left, right, up, or down to add the numbers together to form a "3." The two numbers then become one, freeing up space on the grid for more numbers. You can then combine "3"s to make "6"s and "6"s to make "12"s and so on, doubling up each time for monster scores. Playing is easy, but mastering takes a little bit longer, since you have to know how to maximize your scoring without clogging up the grid and restricting your movement. Once you get the hang of it, the game will become incredibly hard to put down, as all great puzzle games are!

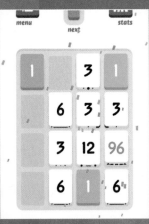

You can see which tile will appear next at the top of the screen, and preview your moves by holding your finger on the screen.

Some cool sound effects and a catchy theme song add a bit of style. The core idea at the heart of *Threes* is good enough that you could do without them, but they add a nice touch of class.

›ALSO CHECK OUT

W.E.L.D.E.R.

WORD

A great puzzle game to test your brain and learn new words at the same time. Slide the lettered tiles to form words, and a built-in dictionary will tell you what they mean.

Words With Friends

W

Challenge your friends in this fun *Scrabble*-like word game where you need to make the highest scoring words you can from the letters you've been dealt. Aim for the bonus tiles to boost your score.

TIPS & TRICKS

WORK THE CORNERS
Try and get your high-scoring tiles close together by restricting your swipes to just two or three directions.

192

DON'T GET DISTRACTED
However tempting it may be to hurry your way to the big matches, try and think ahead and consider the consequences.

START SMALL
It's generally a good idea to start matching small numbered tiles first, before focusing on higher numbers.

Be on the lookout for coins to collect. Not only do these add to your score, they also allow you to unlock bonus power-ups to make subsequent runs much easier.

:::STATS

305,616
is our score to beat

11 UPGRADES
to unlock

3
themed levels

> ## ALSO CHECK OUT

≡ TEMPLE RUN 2

CAN YOU GO THE DISTANCE?

One of the original endless running games to hit the mobile scene, *Temple Run* combined tilt-and-swipe gaming action with a familiar intrepid explorer theme and became an instant classic. This sequel smoothed off some of the sharp edges and incorporated some interesting power-ups, designed to make your runs more profitable in terms of the treasure you collect. Chased out of a temple by some sort of demonic gorilla, your goal is to survive for as long as possible while collecting enough goodies to unlock extra levels and characters. A master class in pick-up-and-play gaming.

Rail Rush
If *Temple Run 2* is like the intro sequence to *Raiders Of The Lost Ark*, then this game is the mine cart sequence from *Temple Of Doom*. Fast and furious on-rails action.

Angry Gran Run
A similar on-rails running game, except this time you play as an angry grandmother as opposed to a dashing explorer. Not as polished as the *Temple Run* games, but still a fun game.

≡ DON'T GET DISTRACTED
If you see a power-up hovering in the air, make sure the path ahead is safe to jump for it. If a hazard approaches, leave it.

≡ MASTER THE MOVE COMBOS
You can go straight from a jump into a slide, and vice versa—handy to know when faced with double hazards later on.

≡ COMPLETE THE CHALLENGES
Take note of the challenges and make a point of completing them. This will send your multipliers through the roof and help you level up quicker.

DESPICABLE ME: MINION RUSH

MINION-THEMED DASHING ACTION

Out of all of the thousands of on-rails running games available for your mobile device, this one ranks among the very best thanks to the sheer amount of fun and variety it serves up. You don't even have to like the Minions to enjoy it (we know the little critters aren't for everyone!), and it presents a genuinely enthralling challenge to test your reflexes. Each dash you undertake has a specific goal that needs completing, but along the way you can collect bananas to spend on gadgets and hit bonus items to play mini-games. It's a lot of fun and super hard to put down.

STATS

750 MILLION
downloads

11 COOL GADGETS
to unlock

26 COSTUMES
to wear

> You must swipe left, right, up, and down to dodge, jump, and slide under oncoming objects that come at you thick and fast.

> ALSO CHECK OUT

Ninja Kid Run
Almost exactly like *Minion Rush* only without all of the blockbuster gimmicks and banana-focused theming. This is a decent alternative to hone your rushing skills.

LEGO Star Wars: The Complete Saga
This awesome LEGO game lets you play through all of the key scenes and battles from the classic *Star Wars* movies and injects plenty of extra humor. It's a LEGO title, but for mobile devices.

TIPS & TRICKS

COLLECT THE BANANAS
Grind out the banana-collecting to purchase upgrades, which can be earned just by playing the game a lot!

UPGRADE WISELY
In the menu you can choose to power up items to help you as you play. You have to spend bananas to do this, so choose carefully.

SAVE THE SERUM
Save the PX41 serum for the toughest challenges. It lets you break through anything in your way.

GLOSSARY

ACCELEROMETER
A tiny chip in your phone or tablet that can recognize small movements of the device. This can be used to control a game, such as steering a car in a racing title.

ANDROID
Google's mobile operating system, which is used on millions of phones around the world.

APP STORE
A virtual store through which you can buy and download apps and games to your devices. For iPhones, this is simply called the App Store. On Android, this is known as the Google Play Store.

ENDLESS RUNNER
A game genre that doesn't have a final point to reach. Your character runs in a never-ending world and the goal is to go the farthest distance or set the highest score.

AUGMENTED REALITY (AR)
Apps that use your device's camera to show an image of the world in front of you, and then overlay game elements (like creatures or items) onto the world.

CODING
The act of writing code. Code is what makes up every computer program and game—learn to code and you can make your own games.

FREE-TO-PLAY (FTP)
Games that are free to download and play, and don't require you to pay any real-world money to enjoy.

FREEMIUM
Freemium titles are free to download, but offer in-app purchases that will allow you to play more easily.

GEOCACHING
When your mobile uses location data to show your position in the real world and reveal items and characters based on that position.

IN-APP PURCHASE
An item you can buy within a game, using real-world money. These can include in-game currency, new characters, and levels, or extra items for characters.

IOS
The operating system used on Apple's iPhone and iPad. This system is only available on Apple's own devices.

IRL
In Real Life.

JRPG
A role-playing game developed in Japan, and often translated into English.

MANAGEMENT SIMULATOR
A game genre in which you oversee and manage many different things at once.

MANA
Characters that can use magic within a game will consume mana as they perform spells. Collecting more mana will recharge their magical powers.

MECH
A large robotic suit that can usually be entered by a human and controlled, giving the character more shielding and more damaging attacks.

METROIDVANIA

A genre of action-adventure game with gameplay concepts similar to the *Metroid* and *Castlevania* series. These games feature large, interconnected worlds, and require players to gain upgrades and new abilities to unlock new areas.

MOTION CONTROLS

A control system that utilizes the accelerometer and other motion sensors that are built into your smartphone or tablet. You can tilt, swing, or shake your device and the game will convert this movement into actions on-screen.

MOD

A modification that changes the way a game is played.

MULTI-TOUCH

Most modern touchscreen devices allow for multi-touch technology. This means you can place two or more fingers on a screen and complete an action to see results in the game.

PAY-TO-WIN

A criticism sometimes leveled at multiplayer games. If a game features in-app purchases that offer powerful weapons, better characters, or extra skills, people who pay to purchase these items have a better chance of winning.

PROCEDURALLY GENERATED

Levels that are created by the game as you play, based on a series of rules and calculations. They will often appear to be quite random, and no two levels will ever be the same.

RHYTHM GAMES

Games that have you tapping in time to music to score points. The better your timing, the higher your score.

ROGUELIKE

A genre of games that typically feature 2-D pixel graphics, a high degree of difficulty, and procedurally generated dungeons. These games are inspired by the 1980 game *Rogue*.

SANDBOX GAME

An area in which the player is given the ability to choose what they do and when. These games often include building and creation aspects, and usually take place in large, open-world environments.

STEAMPUNK

A fantasy world in which advanced steam-powered technology is common. Usually, games in this genre mix old-fashioned styles with powerful computers.

SMARTPHONE

A mobile with a touch-based interface, Internet acces, and an app store. A smartphone combines these features with normal mobile abilities, such as the option to make phone calls.

TABLET

Tablets are often like larger versions of smartphones, but without the same phone capabilities. They have larger screens, and often more powerful processors inside, which can produce better graphics.

TOUCH SCREEN

The main interface used on smartphones and tablets. Most modern touchscreens react to even the softest touches.

TOWER DEFENSE

A game genre that sees onrushing enemies trying to attack and destroy your base. You must place defensive towers strategically to stop the attacking hordes before they reach you.

VIRTUAL D-PAD

A term used to describe the onscreen controls that mobile games often use to help you move characters around the screen.

XP

Experience Points. Gaining enough of these in a game usually results in a character moving to the next skill level and getting better abilities.

VIRTUAL REALITY (VR)

A technology that allows you to place your smartphone in a special headset and hold it up to your eyes. Your phone creates an image for each eye, so it feels like you are looking around the world for real.